YOUNG WRITERS

Spellbound

WARWICKSHIRE

Edited by Sarah Andrew

First published in Great Britain in 1998 by
POETRY NOW YOUNG WRITERS
1-2 Wainman Road, Woodston,
Peterborough, PE2 7BU
Telephone (01733) 230748

HB ISBN 1 86188 890 2
SB ISBN 1 86188 895 3

FOREWORD

In this, our 5th competition year, we are proud to present *Spellbound Warwickshire.* This anthology represents the very best endeavours of the children from this region.

The standard of entries was high, which made the task of editing a difficult one, but nonetheless enjoyable. The variety of subject matter, creativity and imagination never ceases to amaze and is indeed an inspiration to us all.

This year's competition attracted the highest entry ever - over 46,000 from all over the UK, and for the first time included entries from English speaking children living abroad.

Congratulations to all the writers published in *Spellbound Warwickshire.* We hope you enjoy reading the poems and that your success will inspire you to continue writing in the future.

CONTENTS

	Kelly Gudger	1
	Nicola Cartwright	1
Alcester Grammar School		
	Zanitta Hay	2
	Samantha Kibblewhite	2
	Emma Peters	3
	Kay McNamee	4
	Gemma Johnson	4
Alderman Smith School		
	Tegan Harris	5
	Rebecca Alsop	6
	Kimberley Ellis	7
	Andrew Coombs	8
	Amy Ford	9
	Gemma Flower	10
	Amy Ludford	10
	Donna Fessey	11
	Howard Knowles	12
	Gemma Stanton	13
	Sarah Taylor	14
	Phillip Hayes	14
	Kieron Piercy	15
Avon Valley School		
	Kayleigh Waudby	16
	Maria Walton	16
	Carl Israel	17
	David Binns	17
	Tracie Lee	18
	Michelle Bunting	18
	Oliver Green	19
	Neil Jackson & Richard Rippin	20
	Kirsty Grubb	20
	Christopher Dawes	21

Ruth Morris 21
Amy Roberts 22
Rachel O'Meara 22
Stephen Tipple 23
Louise Ward 23
Joanna Grundy 24
Fraser Robinson 24
Donna Hillyard 25
Suzanne Randall 26
Stacey Eccles 26

Etone Community School
Duncan Whittaker 27
Nicola Corby 27
Holly Jones 28
Stephanie Spode 28
Taryn Williams 29
Ian Lungley 30
Ryan Mainwaring 30
Steven Cooper 31
Adam Taylor 31
Rebecca Reed 32
Sarah Cartwright 32
Sarah Tedds 33
Laura Frankcom 34
Craig Muir 34
Esme Townsend 35
Sam Downes 35
Patrick Bell 36
Laura Knighton 37
Lydia Collins 37
Lucie Bevins 38
Martyn Moreno-Melgar 39
Rachel Galland 39
Rebecca Jackson 40
Michael Dore 40
Gemma Waring 41
Mark Williams 42

Rebecca Hibbins 42
Daniel Fletcher 43
Thomas Cheffings 44
Neshol Patel 44
Nicola Cartwright 45
Mark Styles 45
Chris Smart 46
Lisa Hall 46
David Evans 47
Merissa Bend 48
Abigail Leadbeater 48
Kerry Kendall 49
Kirstie Willis 49
Gemma Hyde 50
Sarah Garside 50
Robert Turner 51
Kiran Grigg 51
Lindsey Ridgway 52
Nathan Gilliver 52
Nicola Machin 53
Claire Rowley 53
Sara Stubbs 54
Sean Crashley 55

George Eliot School

Charlotte Courtney 56
Terri-Marie Lewis 57
Charlotte Lathbury 57
Kristine Bradley 58
Sarah Clarke 58
Gemma Goode 59
Meera Rathod 59
Alex McDonald 60
Oi Ka Law 60
John Quinney 61
Andy Vernon 62
Claire Huxley 62
Scott Friswell 63

Zoe Averns 64

Hartshill School

Ellen Phillips 64
Tom Marshall 65
Louise Owens 65
Kelly Gudger 66
Hayley Biddle 66
Lindsay Hall 67
Graeme Gudger 67
Cheryl Fox 68
Amy Jayne Matts 68
Aaron Sheridan 69
Adam Brown 69
Kate Marshall 70
Darren Brown 71
Samuel Hands 71
Louise Brown 72
Kevin Jones 72
Emma Elverson 73
Gemma McLeod 73
Kerry Hamilton 74
Scott Osborne 75
Carl Hutchinson 75
James Barr 76
Colin Straker 76
Leigh Stallard 77
Janine Turvey 77
Charlotte Brindley 78
Jennifer Bucknall 78
Elaine Brown 79
Kate Brown 79
Janine Turvey 80
Ryan Stuart Ashby 80
Natalie Osadciw 81
Tanneke De Vogel 81
Mathew Stanley 82
Daren Eggleton 82

Sammy Lee	83
Rachael Beardall	84
James Percival	84
Charlotte Ann Croft	85
Michael Elkin	85
Jade Paintin	86
Joanne Short	86
Lorna Tarplin	87
Lucy Carne	87
Melissa Day	88
Nicola Ashtiaq	88
Helen Holt	89
James Rathbone	89
Juliet Reeves-Eastwood	90
Nicola Hadley	91
Emma Ashby	92
Adam Robinson	92
Victoria Ward	93
Scott McEwan	93
Nicole Cleave	94
Christopher Martin	94
Rebecca Campbell	95
Elliot Caddy	95
Alison Aucott	96
Jenna Haldane	96
Emily Arkinstall	97
Emma Harris	97
Zac Davies	98
Sam Essex	98
James Everard	99
Natasha Perkins	99
Aimee Oakley	100
Sarah Morris	100
Matthew Potter	101
Dean Pate	101
Kirsty Miles	102
Luke Beardmore	102
Rebecca Lewis	103

Kevin Mullins 103
Laura Stringer 104
Kent W Dwyer 104
Katie Brookes 105
Claire Doughty 105
Louise Chérif 106
Jonathan Young 106
James Ritchie 107
Terry Paul 107
Laura Ashby 108
Matthew Glover 108
Neil Percival 109
Samantha Swami 109
Kelly Greenaway 110
Lee Straker 110
Nikki Owen 111
Jamie Steggles & Richard Gazeley 112
Matthew Sears 112
Vicky Whopples 113
Gemma Morton & Bernadette Arnold 113
Thomas Essex 114
Claire Benford 114
Shelley Morris 115
Emma Sugars 115
Siân Corbett 116
Thomas Percival 116
Elizabeth King 117
Jon Zeslawski 117
Amanda Thomas 118
Stephanie Jack 118
Marc Gilbey & Matthew Hatcher 119
Shaun Philbin 119
Helen Morris 120
Colin Straker 120
Nimmy Ayilara 121
Kieran Brennan 121
Natalie Eggison 122
Tara Osborne 122

Robert Morris	123
Thomas Jones	123
Charlotte Dyde	124
Lesley Mara	124
David McLoughlin	125
Ashan Chaudry	125
Jody Hughes	126
Danielle Clark	126
Louisa Haddon	127
Kirk Devlin	127
Jamie Rana	128
Ammie Stringer	128
Chris Skilling	129
Kerrie Dickens	129
Ian Parker	130
Chris Sadler	130
Barry Roberts	130
Chris Phipps	131
Amy Owen	131
Gordon & Marcus	132
Rebecca Ewing	132
Carl Fox	133
Ellen Curry	133
James Dunn	134
Nick Spittle	134
Lisa Bromley	134
Kylie White	135
Gareth Robinson	135
Pascal Grant	136
Katie Morrison	136
Beverley Johnson	137
Sarah Keeling	137
David Garrett	138
Rachel Coles	138
Laura Jayne Marshall	139
Gary Hughes	139

Higham Lane School

	Elizabeth Sidwell	140
	Marie Nickels	140
	Hannah Williams	141
	Anjaljeet Sandhu	141
	Nikki Ind	142
	Laura Lee	143
	David Helps	144
	Fiona Morris	145

Hillcrest School

	Nadia Mubarak	145

Kenilworth School

	Laura Hanley-Gorton	146
	Hannah Merry	146
	Lisa Clifton	147
	Sophie Hunter	147
	Joanne Naylor	148
	Laura Bailey	148
	Laura Evans	149
	Hannah Walter	150
	Lyndsey Gallagher	150
	Kate Holmes	151
	Vicky Hill	151
	Leona Archer	152
	Chloe M Dore	153
	Amit Bagga	154

St Benedict's RC High School

	Benedict Peters	154
	Claire Dawes	155
	Claire Hodgets	156
	Janine Czaplinska	157
	Katie Thurlow	158
	Leisha Rymsza	159
	Katie Summers	160
	Claire Wright	161

Hannah Baker 162
Paul Freeman 163
Mark Moulder 163
David Barrett 164
Oliver Mansbridge 164
Guy Barlow 165
Kathy McGreal 166
Amy Flint 166
Mark Thompson 167
Cheryl Hathaway 168

St Joseph's School

Kimberley Hiles 169
Amandeep Johal 170
Penny Smith 171
Narelle Callaghan 171
Alex Wagstaff 172
Natasha Jeffs 172
Carolyn Bradley-Winnett 173
Lucy Greville-Smith 173
Sarah Warn 174
Maria Murray 174
Emily Murden 175
Emily Farley 175
Amy Browne 176
Jackie Little 176
Amanda Rees 177
Kelly Louden 178
Stephanie Laird 179
Catherine Tressler 180
Katherine Shaw 181
Katy Bennett 182

Southam High School

Stephanie Brown 183
Alison Jackson 183
Carla Iliffe 184
Gemma Florida 184

] Carly Allum 185
Adam Wilson 185
Sarah Talbot 186
Sarah Glover 186
Simon Dommett 187
David Rowley 187
Nicholas Holland 188
Rob Milburn 188
Laura Rawlings 189
Adam Smith 189
] Hannah Lee 190
Samantha Meredith 190
Becky Busby 191
Samantha Cowley 191
Gemma Reeves 192
Alison Morris 192
Liz Bench 193
John Perry 193
Zoe Carroll 194
John-Paul Ellis 194
Catherine Priest 195
Natalie Rabôt 196
Shanne Rawbone 196
Sam Cronin 197
Dan Houghton 197
Sharon Joyce 198
Luke Facer 199
Chris Corkhill 199
Coral Tassi 200
Becky Bennett 200
Abby Pink 201
David Waddell 202
Ashley Hancock 202
Alie Green 203
Samantha Godfrey 203
Alan Amaira 204
Kieren Bodill 204
Lucy Beeston 205

Tim Welby 206
Matt Hill 207
Mark Higgs 207
Charlotte Rudge 208
Katie Alsop 209
Deborah Williams 210
Alan Guilford 211
Rachel Wandod 212

Sparrowdale School

Samantha Rowley 213
Stevan Ptaszynski 213
Matthew Mitchell 214
Anna-Marie Cheshire 214
Steven Cousins 214

Stratford High School

Katie Shelton-Smith 215
Amy Bishop 216
Kate Harrison 216
Lisa Fernandes 217
Charlotte Pearce 218
Emma Jones 218
Katherine Latham 219
Ella Selwood 220
Lisa Griffiths 221
Nikki Jennings 221
Becky Caden 222
Nicola Sach 223
Gareth Ridgley 224
Amiee Cotterill 224
David Podmore 225
Michael Wood 225
Scott Redhead 226
Ian Terry 226
Gemma Gold 227
Jodie Vest 228
Stewart Crow 229

Nicholas Osman	229
Simon Walton	230
Adam Martin	230
Oliver Stewart	231
Katie Walter	232
Claire May	232
Melantha Thomson	233
David Eburah	233
Ingram Hazel	234
Lydia Burton	235
Natalie Kemp	235
Gemma Caldwell	236
Timothy Woolley	236
Phoebe English	237
Sophie Leow-Dyke	237
Sian Haggitt	238
Aaron Aston	238
Steven Perkins	239
Sara Franklin	239
Siân Walters	240
Becky Tucker	241
Martin Baxter	242
Benjamin Skinner	243
Alicia Leow-Dyke	243
Johanna Holdsworth	244
Amanda Keech	244
Katie Chandler	245
Kelly Millward	246
Chris Wood	246
Gemma Hawkins	247
Zoe Russon	247
Martha Welch	248
Gemma Crow	248
Lisa Grasby	249
Joe Evans	249
Laura Collins	250
Sam Lee	250
Hannah Wilson	251

Esther Foster 252
Elizabeth Blewer 252
Hannah Whatcott 253
Liane Garside 254
Robbie Parker 254
Amy Wein 255
Kerry Ford 256
Stephen Devey 256
Hayley Ash 257
Rachel Day 257
Kelly Nicholls 258
Sophie Lemberger 259
Phillip Camp 260
Helen Goodman 260
Sara Casley 261
Tom Cox 262
Michael Scowcroft 262
Joanne Dyer 263
Gemma Newby 264
Michael Bush 264
Nikola Hamer 265
Rick Frier 265
Lauren Dyer 266
Ruth Woodward 266
Hannah Rowland 267

THE POEMS

Will Always Shine

Have you ever noticed how
The stars shine so bright
And whenever you're doing something wrong
At the time it seems to be right.
If you ever feel sad
Always say that you are fine
Because even on a rainy day
Some sun always has to shine.
Sometimes you are never happy
Not even a bit
But somewhere in your heart of hearts
A flame will always be lit.

Kelly Gudger (13)

The Beginning Of Spring

The butterfly flutters along,
Following the bird as he sings his song,
The sun shines high in the sky,
While the breeze gives a gentle sigh,
The trees gently nod their heads,
While flowers sleep in their beds,
The blackbird begins to sing,
To celebrate the first day of spring.

Nicola Cartwright (13)

A Lost Soul

She built a wall around herself,
Blacked out her mind to the pain she felt,
She carved a mask that time hollowed out,
She doesn't know what made her happiness melt,
But she knows that her cards have all been dealt,
And she knows she's got the back of the belt,
And she doesn't know why,
But she knows she'll get by,
And she tries and she tries,
Then she stops,
Then she sighs,
And she starts to cry,
She's back under the spell she thought she had broke,
And she's gotta realise that this is no joke,
Then just as fast as it was gone,
She's picked up the mask and put it back on,
Then slowly,
So slowly,
She turns,
And is gone.

Zanitta Hay (14)
Alcester Grammar School

Why Me?

Why is it me they bully?
Why is it me they attack?
Why is it me they pin to the wall
and punch till my eyes are black?

Why every morning when I awake
do I wish it would still be night?
Why when I get dressed for school
do I find myself trembling with fright?

Why when I'm clever at lessons
is it playtimes they force me to hate?
Why do I linger at hometime?
Are they waiting for me at the gate?

Why are school days a problem?
Why do they fill me with dread?
Why do I bother living
when I think I'd be better off dead?

Samantha Kibblewhite (11)
Alcester Grammar School

PANDA'S PREDICAMENT

Please protect me
My family's getting very small,
Destroying my habitat isn't necessary
So why do you do it at all?

We're not just cuddly toys you know
This world is ours as much as yours.
Give our young a chance to grow
Let's hear the patter of tiny paws.

So when you see a picture of me
Don't just say 'Ah that's cute.'
Join a campaign deliver our plea
Don't destroy, don't endanger, don't pollute.

Emma Peters (11)
Alcester Grammar School

Fight Or Flight?

Do we respect or do we fear
Those who assemble us and tell us right
From wrong?
For five long years I battled with Mephistopheles.
I lost.
So turned me to paper, and
Left me to flutter on the breeze.
That is, until
I saw the reflected despair of the Exile,
And the Rock Limpet clung to me.
Then I realised - it's not so bad
Because
Death might have been my beginning, and
Death will be my living,
From now on I will live until I die.

Kay McNamee (16)
Alcester Grammar School

The Pessimist's Dream

As I look up to the sky,
I wonder why it is so high;
How can a person like me try
To reach my dreams.

I have not the strength enough;
The road looks smooth but it is rough.
I should have seen it would be tough
To reach my dreams.

I struggle up, yet down I drop,
Like a balloon, soon I shall pop,
Will I ever reach the top?
To reach my dreams.

Even though the world was hard,
And I couldn't see what was on the cards,
I've overcome the final yard;
I've reached my dreams.

Gemma Johnson (14)
Alcester Grammar School

A Lucky Wish

Yesterday towards the end of day,
I found a small cat litter tray,
I found it lying next to the drain
It's dirty through lying in the rain.
Today right behind dad's garden shed
Where tools lie scattered, as though dead,
I found a tiny, cute little bowl
And it's almost a perfect whole.
This for me has been a lucky week,
Think, it would be a real big cheek
To wish to find a little kitten?
Love it lots and call it 'Dicken'.
I'd cherish it as my very own,
And keep it safe within my home.
Oh haven't I been really lucky?
Before the week is really through,
Fingers crossed that my wish will come true.

Tegan Harris (12)
Alderman Smith School

SUMMER'S HERE

Summer's here,
Spring's gone.
I like summer,
It is fun.

I go on holiday,
To see the sea and sand.
It is very hot,
But oh, so grand.

I dig in the sand,
And swim in the sea.
I love the hot weather,
But, ouch! I get stung by a bee!

I smell the salt water,
When I'm in the sea.
The sun is shining,
Down on me.

It's time to go,
I don't want to yet.
But I have to,
As the sun's nearly set.

Rebecca Alsop (12)
Alderman Smith School

SPELLBOUND!

My garden gnomes always whizz whirl and
swirl away, count to three and go away,
but come back another day.
Molly Holly and Wally all come
back the next day.
But they had all disappeared, they were
nowhere to be seen.
I went to go and find them,
I went along by the shops it wasn't too
many stops.
I went to the park by now the
park was dark.
I saw spider on the way he had
some new shoes he was going to show
the kangaroos.
I then decided to go back home
so I went on the bus it wasn't too
much fuss.
I bumped into mouse before
entering the house.
As I walked in the blue-eyed cat was
sitting on her mat, she saw a bat
but was way too fat to catch the bat.

Kimberley Ellis (12)
Alderman Smith School

DRAGONS

Up in the clouds
or the clear blue sky
dragons come out to have a fly.

There's two at the front
with big red tails
and the rest at home at the speed of snails.

They twist and turn
and spin and dive
and one says it's what keeps him alive.

When most have been and had their fun
they turn around
to go back to mum.

Their mother is big and bold
and most say
she's got a heart of gold.

When they get home it's time for tea
they ate honey sandwiches
from a flying bee.

After that they go out and about
to dance and sing
and jump and shout.

Children be quiet
and play my game
now who can breathe the longest flame?

They took a deep breath
until they were loaded
and then blew out and the cave exploded.

'Oh you naughty dragons,' mother said
'you've burnt down the curtains
and singed Uncle Ted.'

Andrew Coombs (12)
Alderman Smith School

THE QUEEN OF HEARTS

Where did the time go?
If only someone was to know
That her life would be cut short.
All her life she fought
To help someone else, to help another
And for Will and Harry, to be a good mother.
She died and it was not deserved
But her place in heaven was reserved.
A world in mourning
Yet another day is dawning
Her life is now a legend
Never to be forgotten.
She will live on in our hearts forever
And that was her true life's ambition
Which she has now fulfilled.
She can now rest in peace watching over us
The Queen of our hearts
And the caring mother of us all.

Amy Ford (12)
Alderman Smith School

WALKING AT NIGHT

It's 8 o'clock and
I'm out for a walk,
The wind passes through
my voice as I talk.
The cold wind swifts
round my nose and
then it goes right
down to my toes.
The trees sway slowly
and the leaves fall off,
the street lamps
come on and then
the cold makes me cough.
My footsteps get silent
in the crisp green grass,
as the cold hits my face . . .
. . . I let out a gasp.

Gemma Flower (12)
Alderman Smith School

SOUND!

The piccolo's sharp, whistling sound,
Is enough to put anybody on the edge of their seats,
It sounds like an angry mother bird who has seen a cat.

The flute's gentle and graceful sound,
Is played with great emotion and care,
It sounds like it is a gentle breeze blowing through wind chimes,
When you play the flute you can feel the music run through you.

The saxophone's deep, low voice,
Is like a child running wild through the streets,
The saxophone you have to play with skill and confidence,
You blow the music out but it talks to you in your mind.

The clarinet's deep-winded sound,
Blows across the nation without a care,
Carrying its music as it travels through the air,
As the clarinet travels through your body you feel emotion and joy.

Amy Ludford (12)
Alderman Smith School

THE OLD EMPTY HOUSE

There's an old empty house as weird as can be
Creepy and cold and scaring me.
Rats, bats and flying cats hidden in traps
Plants, water and wind all falling in.
In the dark dark corner of the dark dark windows
There's cobwebs and nests with all birds in.

Hidden passageways behind book shelves
Spooky ghosts running through the halls
passageways and through doors.
Moss climbing up the walls and do you
know what they say 'Oh what a fright'
with delight.
At night it's like the middle of nowhere
There's a dark dark room and no one's been in it.
It's too gloomy.

Donna Fessey (12)
Alderman Smith School

FOOD

I love my food
my gorgeous gorgeous food
It's yummy
and really really scrummy.

Chocolate flake
and chocolate mousse
and a chocolate bean
is all you need.

I love lollies
the shape of dollies
blue ones red ones
pink ones too.

I love chips
as big as battleships
greasy ones fatty ones
and salty ones too.

I love my food
my gorgeous gorgeous food
it's yummy
and really really scrummy.

Howard Knowles (12)
Alderman Smith School

GOLDEN DOVE

The tears that flow for you
would make a river wide.
The emotions that we feel for you
will never be set aside.
The tragedy that fell upon you
fell upon us too.
Our hearts are all now broken
for the love of you.
The tears and fears that we pray
will slowly start to
fade away.
The strength and compassion
you gave to us
and taught throughout the land
has now made us
so much stronger to help
love and understand.
Although your death was tragic
it was not at all in vain.
It has made us all one nation brought
together through our pain.
As we light the candles in your memory
you fly above like a golden dove.
The candle's burnt out long before your legend
ever will.

Gemma Stanton (12)
Alderman Smith School

Our Queen Of Hearts!

Our Queen of Hearts
Had to part,
with those she loved the most,
We all boast about how much
we love and care,
Right from the start to the time
for us to part!

She helped and cared for those in need,
Even those who need a feed!
We love you Diana,
So much indeed!

Goodbye forever friend
From all those in need
We miss you a lot,
'The world's best friend!'

Sarah Taylor (12)
Alderman Smith School

The Dolphin

I wish I was a dolphin
to swim in the sea
gliding along just feeling free

No cars, no aeroplanes,
No people to see
Just lots of clear water
and real friends with me

With the clear blue sky
and the satin sea
I wish I was a dolphin
to be at peace in the sea.

Phillip Hayes (12)
Alderman Smith School

FOOTBALL FOOTBALL

United chasing for the title
Cov are fighting for survival
Wrighty fighting with the ball
at the moment his chance is very small
That he might get it in the net
Here comes Giggsy he's a threat
Giggs running down the wing
as the crowd start to sing

Oh no it's too late
All the fans have pushed down the gate
Oh no they've started a riot!
Now the crowd have gone really quiet
Huckaby in with a shot,
Oops too late Schmeichel's got!

Football it's turned into a war
but the crowd still ask for more
Forty pound for a shirt!
Oh a foul that's got to hurt
Oh it's Beckham what a goal
Football is the lads' heart and soul.

Kieron Piercy (12)
Alderman Smith School

WHAT IS HALLOWE'EN?

What is Hallowe'en
Really what does this mean?
Scary spiders jumping about
Spooky ghosts popping out
Witches riding on broomsticks high
Right up there in the dark night sky
Haunting noises sound and shrill
Black cauldrons steaming
Ready to fill.
A little black cat beside it there
Waiting for its next big scare
Hallowe'en sure sounds fun
But if anyone frightens me . . .
Watch me run!

Kayleigh Waudby (11)
Avon Valley School

HALLOWE'EN THING

Ghosts in sheets,
dance along the streets,
Witches on broomsticks,
With their black cats play tricks,
Hallowe'en is a scary night
When people dressed up can
give you a fright,
You get an apple or more,
when you knock upon a door,
Shouting trick or treat,
When someone opens it
they give you a sweet.

Maria Walton (12)
Avon Valley School

THE RAZOR BROTHERS

Whether you're good
Whether you're not
Whether you stand
Whether you drop
Whether you sit
Whether you slide
Whether you die
Whether you stay alive
Whether you've got Havoc Cozmos or
Sanate.
Whether you can jump your wall or your
garden gate.
Whether you've got Bauer Roces
or trades
It don't really matter you've got
some blades.

Carl Israel (14)
Avon Valley School

THE MUTTERINGS OF DR FRANKENSTEIN

Frankenstein muttered to himself
Whilst slime dripped from the shelf.
'Vampires and bats are all very well
for the average spooky land,
but if I invented bigger monsters,
Oh boy! Wouldn't it be grand.'

David Binns (11)
Avon Valley School

Trick Or Treat

Hallowe'en comes every year.
Celebrating the beginning
of winter.

People wearing frightening masks,
go trick or treating.
Children in white gowns
with skeleton faces
walk carrying Jack-o'-lanterns.
Fires burn, witches
and black cats creep.
Ghosts and ghouls, haunt
the streets.
Wolves howl as the
night nears in.
At midnight all is calm
and black, but the moon
still shines.

Tracie Lee (11)
Avon Valley School

I Love Him To Bits

I love his hair
It's full of colour
Every time I see him
My heart feels fuller

I stare into his eyes
They are so sweet
Everything about him is perfect
Even down to his feet

I sit with him
In his company for hours
He is so cute and
Seems to have special loving powers

I know he loves me too
Being with him becomes a habit
I brush his lovely brown fur
Yes I love Smudge my pet rabbit.

Michelle Bunting (13)
Avon Valley School

School Days

'S chool days', they say that they're your best, but
what would they know.
C an't they see that you hate it and don't want to go.
H orrible! That's what they are. Every day they send
me to that place. And I hate it.
O h they can't understand, they must have got treated
differently in the 'Stone age'.
O ver and over the same lessons every day.
L essons, lessons why oh why, can't we just stay
at home by the telly.

D ays on end, I sit starring at the white board
with a voice somewhere in the distance.
A ll I have learnt is fractions, where Africa is and
when King George the 3rd was born.
Y es, I've got a plan, I'm going to run away then I won't have
to go at all.
S o I'll run. No I won't I've said that before. I guess
I'll just go to school another day.

Oliver Green (14)
Avon Valley School

VIOLENCE

Late at night walking through the street,
Turn the corner, but who do you meet?
A big gang, ready to give you a beat,

You get punched in the nose kicked in the head,
Lying there for hours thinking you're dead.

Wake up in the morning wanting to cry,
choosing whether you live or die.

The ambulance is here, your parents arrive,
All that you say is you were learning to drive.

You haven't got a car, how could that be,
that's it boy you're staying with me.

Oh my God, I'm in for it now, they'll never understand,
nowhere, nohow.

Neil Jackson & Richard Rippin (13)
Avon Valley School

SMELL MY FEET

Trick or treat smell my feet
Give me something good to eat
Candy or sweet I do not care
Give me something that I could share
With ghosts and goblins I do not care
Just kindly give me something
that I could share!

Kirsty Grubb (11)
Avon Valley School

GRINNING BATS

I n the dead of night,
T he bats cry with laughter

L ate people who were going
home become early meals.
A fter the bite there
is no hope!
U nknowing that you could
be next
G od can't help you.
H ell could be round
the next corner.
S urrounding the prey,
the prey is you!

Christopher Dawes (12)
Avon Valley School

TRAMPOLINING

T earing through the air,
R ound and round like a merry-go-round,
A nd then nearly falling down,
M ore and more, I enjoy it much more.
P osing on the trampoline.
O h no! I've fallen off.
L ying on the floor.
I n a second I'm up again.
N o one's really laughing.
I 'm alright though.
N ow I've got to get back on,
G ong! The bell goes it's time to get off.

Ruth Morris (13)
Avon Valley School

BULLYING

Bullies, why do they do it?
for fun, for laughter,
They think it's a game,
To others it's torture.

They kick you,
They hit you,
They think it's a laugh
You beg, you plead,
Why won't they stop?

All the names,
All the sadness,
One day it'll stop,
One day it'll end.

Amy Roberts (13)
Avon Valley School

OH I LOVE HIM

Oh I love him,
His deep blue eyes,
His dark, soft black hair.
Come upstairs I say to him,
Come and see my room,
We snuggle up together in bed,
Oh he's so soft and cuddly,
His warm body pressed against
mine
Oh I love him,
My pet cat Chip!

Rachel O'Meara (13)
Avon Valley School

If I Had Lots Of Money

If I had lots of money
I'd buy myself a car,
Or maybe lots of sporty shops
Or even a gold bar.

If I had lots of money
I'd buy myself a house,
With a massive TV set
And my own pet mouse.

If I had lots of money
I wouldn't know what to buy first,
It would drive me completely nuts
My brain would suddenly burst.

If I had lots of money
I'd go completely mad,
I think I'll stick with being poor
Like a normal lad.

Stephen Tipple (13)
Avon Valley School

Harvest Time

H arvest time is here again
A ray of blinding sun
R ed glowing golden leaves
V ibrant colours all around
E veryone is happy everywhere we go
S heaves of corn swaying in the wind
T his proves that autumn's here.

Louise Ward (14)
Avon Valley School

TV . . .

It's something that I live for.
Something that I'd die without.
It's in every house, eyes see it with delight,
Knowing they *will* stay in tonight.
In the morning the news is on. Just by
watching it you know what's going on
halfway round the world and back.
When they're in school or at work that's
all they think about, watching it.
The horror, the comedy, music and action
It's all there.
Every night when they come home they all see it,
Eyes watch its every moving motion.
You have one small or big, it brings a smile to your face.
But that's not all . . .

Joanna Grundy (13)
Avon Valley School

EVIL NIGHT COMES WITH A FRIGHT

Hallowe'en comes once a year,
Ghosts and ghouls, all that fear.
Things that go bump in the night,
Guaranteed to give us a fright.

Skeletons rising at their will,
Sending shivers that would chill.
Things are crawling in them ditches,
So beware there's also witches.

Zombies, Freddie Kruger and Candyman,
Trying to scare us as much as they can.
All those things will make you shout,
So take my advice and don't go out.

Fraser Robinson (11)
Avon Valley School

Witches' Potion

They swoop in the night,
on a stick made of wood,
and a woman, a cat who
likes wearing black.
A potion they made with an
old frog's back, spiders' legs,
and an old smelly sock.
Bats' brains, frog nails
old whales, slimy snails.

This potion they made was
for headaches and pains.
The witch gave it to her
cat which never woke again.

Donna Hillyard (11)
Avon Valley School

BULLYING

You're fat
You're ugly
You're thick and dumb
You're a cow
You're a pig
Say it say it
I'm fat
I'm ugly
I'm thick and dumb
I'm a cow
I'm a pig
I'm strong
I'm hard
I stand up to my troubles
But what about you?

Suzanne Randall (13)
Avon Valley School

POETRY COMPETITION

We're here again another day,
It's cold outside why do we have to stay?
I've been at school since I was four,
Will I ever see the door?
Maths, English, science and tech,
All my books are a wreck,
All the teachers do is shout,
Telling us to get out.
Shut up, get out, we are always
getting told,
Those words are really, really old.

Stacey Eccles (13)
Avon Valley School

The Little Dickybird

One little dickybird
Sitting in the road
Along came a car
And broke its every bone
Along came the cat
And punched him in the face
Knocked the little birdy
Into outer space.
The birdy came down
And landed on the cat
The cat ran away
So birdy laughed
All day.

Duncan Whittaker (11)
Etone Community School

Decorating

I'm having double glazing,
It is really amazing,
I've never had it before,
I'm also having a new door,
My old windows are really boring,
They have no colour to them in the morning.

Did you know how much this costs,
Believe me a lot of dosh,
We're having diamonds which are meant
to be better than squares,
Because they match the carpet on
the stairs.

Nicola Corby (12)
Etone Community School

EMOTIONS

He's winning
She's losing
He's shouting
She's boozing

He's happy
She's sad
He's good
She's bad

He's rich
She's poor
He's contented
She wants more

He's light
She's dark

Together they combine
Together they make my
mind.

Holly Jones (13)
Etone Community School

LIFE

Every day I ask myself,
What's the point in life?
Getting up, ready for school,
It is my daily ritual.

One day I'll be old enough,
To do just as I want,
Going out, hanging around,
Anything will be alright.

Then I'll be even older,
Unable to do a thing.
Sitting in an old comfy chair,
With my family all around me.

I will look upon my childhood,
As if it was yesterday
But deep down inside I'll know,
Yesterday has passed and died.

Stephanie Spode (13)
Etone Community School

HELP MY CAT'S ON FIRE!

He's playing ever so playfully
But little does he know
The fire is right behind him
And he's wagging his tail right by it.
A flame jumps out and catches him
Right on the tip of his tail
Help! My cat's on fire
And now he's started to wail
He's running round in circles
Very, very fast
He's trying to catch the flame
But he burns his mouth instead
He's rolling up and down the floor
But the carpet sets alight
His ears have two flame earrings
He's going up in smoke
And now he's covered in water
And looks like a drowned rat
He's nearly bald but black
And he started off as white.

Taryn Williams (13)
Etone Community School

Football

Out on the pitch
Twenty-two players trying to score

Giving away penalties
and free kicks

Signing autographs for people

Either winning or losing.

Getting medals and cups

Playing other teams

Coach shouting loud

Dribbling and shooting

That's football.

Ian Lungley (11)
Etone Community School

Man United

M anchester United
A re the best.
N ever losing to the rest.

U nder pressure that don't matter.
T aking victories is what they do best.
D efending well is what they're good at.

Ryan Mainwaring (13)
Etone Community School

Seasons

Spring is a time to get on your vest,
To lie on the grass and let the sun do the rest.
The lambs are born and the birds start to sing,
The daffodils open what a beautiful thing.
Summer is a time for the flowers to bloom,
This is the time when a bride wants a groom.
The church bells ring and the sun it glows,
This is the time when everything grows.
Autumn is the time when the wind blows strong,
The days are short and the nights are long.
When the leaves are brown and they start to fall,
You know that Christmas isn't far at all.
Winter is a time for rain and snow,
Everyone shops and their noses glow.
Christmas is near and all the children cheer,
Mums make dinner and the dads drink beer.

Steven Cooper (11)
Etone Community School

Ants

Hungry ants
Scavenging in the dark ditches
Sheltering
From the clinging rain
Splashing on the
Slushed
Muddy
Ground,
Washing the ants away.

Adam Taylor (12)
Etone Community School

BULLY

Do you like to see me sad?
Head bowed down and tears in my eyes.
Why do you hurt me with your hatred?
Why do you tell me lies?

Do you want to see me hurt?
Tears falling as I cry.
Making me dread each day,
Making me wish I'd die.

Can't you let me live my life?
When you're around I feel fear,
When you try to hurt me,
My smiles turn into tears.

These bruises you have given me,
I have tried to hide,
On the outside I am smiling,
But the pain is deep inside.

Rebecca Reed (12)
Etone Community School

PRECIOUS

Jumping on tables, climbing on chairs.
Doing things that no other cat dares.
Staring at goldfish in their bowl
Peeping at mice in their hole.
Though not all the time is he bad
Sometimes I'm quite smitten
By Precious my little kitten.

Sarah Cartwright (11)
Etone Community School

My Pet The Little Pest

My pet dog,
Is a little pest,
She never sits down,
Or has a rest.

Upstairs, downstairs,
all around,
Chewing things,
that she has found.

Taken her for a walk,
at the local park,
Chasing, running, playing,
Oh! What a lark.

In the garden,
Digging holes,
Big ones, small ones,
Lots to hide.

Is it a shoe?
Is it a bone?
No one really knows.

Night has come,
bed at last,
Dreams of bones,
And killing cats.

Sarah Tedds (12)
Etone Community School

Food Is Good

One day we'll all grow old, year by year
day by day
But first we'll eat plenty of food
Starfish strawberries lemons and limes
They're also healthy we'll all be fine

Bananas oranges apples and pears
Peaches plums all are fine.
Healthy eating is what we're told
But mixed together we'll grow old

Chips, sweets, spuds and chocolate
These are the things we've eaten
Chips beans and chicken all mixed
Together can be a good daily dish.

Laura Frankcom (12)
Etone Community School

I Love Fishing

I love fishing
big fish little fish
carp, roach
perch, pike

Fishing is fun
fishing is great every day

I love fishing
Mum hates it
I don't care what
anybody says 'cos
I love fishing.

Craig Muir (12)
Etone Community School

MOLE

I need help,
So help me,
I'm a mole,
You're a mouse,
I'm in a hole,
You're in a house,
I can't see,
And you can,
That is why I need you;

Here I come,
There you are,
Dressed in white,
Dressed in grey,
At last you've seen the light of day,
Now you must come out to play.

Esme Townsend (11)
Etone Community School

LOST

I look all around me but who can I see?
I see no one but me
I look in the mirror but who do I see?
I see no one but me
I go to the park but who do I see?
I see no one but me
I must be lost
No one's there
I'm all alone but who cares?

Sam Downes (12)
Etone Community School

ME

Sometimes I am angry
Sometimes I am mad
Sometimes I am quiet
Sometimes I am sad

When I get angry
I punch kick and swear
I hurt lots of people
and I don't really care

When I get mad
I throw things on the floor
I shout out stupid things
and I slam my bedroom door

When I am quiet,
I'm thinking what I've done
If I didn't do these things
I would have much more fun

When I am sad
I want to make things right
I'd really like a cuddle
I don't want to fight

I want to change
I'll do my best
I want to be just
like the rest.

Patrick Bell (12)
Etone Community School

I LOVE MY PONY CONKER

I love my pony Conker.
He means so much to me.
Carrots, apples, Polos
He loves all three.
I love the way he gallops
I love the way he trots.
but either way I still love him a lot.

I love my pony Conker
The way he jumps around
His chestnut ears are beautiful
His wildness goes all round.

I love my pony Conker
His coat gleams so much.
He has a lovely white patch.
No other can match.

I love my pony Conker
But now it's time to go
His saddle's on, his girth is tight
Now it's time to ride.

Laura Knighton (12)
Etone Community School

ZOE!

I know a little girl
Who is as bright as rain,
But above all she's a little pain,
She storms off in a mood
And shouts (I don't like you)
But it's OK as she's only three.

Lydia Collins (13)
Etone Community School

BULLYING

It happens in the playground
It happens in the loo
They wait outside the school gate,
Just to pick on you.

They torment you, taunt you
Call you names
Pick on you, make you cry,
Not letting you join in any games.

It happens at the bus stop,
It happens in the class
They always know the right time,
No adults walking past.

Push you, pull you
Nip you and squeeze
Saying cruel things just to tease.

It happens in the corridor
It happens in the yard
They used to be your pals once
Now they hit you hard.

They take your crisps, sweets and money
laughing, laughing, thinking it's funny.
It happens all the time
No one's ever there to see
But what I'd like to know is
Why's it always me . . . ?

Lucie Bevins (11)
Etone Community School

HOMEWORK

I hate homework
It's very very sad
Sitting at the table
It makes me very mad
Can't watch the telly
Which makes me feel bad
English is OK
Maths is yuck!
Science is cool
But the homework sucks
I've finished my homework
I'm very very glad
Now I can watch telly
Or have a little nap.

Martyn Moreno-Melgar (110
Etone Community School

SUMMER HOLIDAYS

Summer is a nice time of the year,
We go on our holidays and dad drinks lots of beer,
We go on the beach with our buckets and spades,
And dig some holes and bury ourselves,
We go to buy some chips,
And sit by the harbour and watch the ships,
The seagulls fly past,
They flap their wings and move very fast,
But soon the fun will be over,
Back home to sail to Dover.

Rachel Galland (11)
Etone Community School

CHRISTMAS EVE

The tree stands alone in the corner,
 Waiting to be dressed.
With baubles, candles, tinsel and lights,
 Just waiting to impress.

The children place their chocolates,
 Upon the tree so tall.
The gifts they wrap with ribbons and bows,
 They place beneath for all.

At night they sing their carols,
 Which are sung so merrily.
They dance and laugh and then they have,
 Mulled wine and mince pies for tea.

The evening now draws to a close,
 Let's go to sleep they said.
It's time for Santa to visit them,
 All tucked up warm in bed.

They do not hear the jingling,
 of the sledge upon the roof.
But we all know that Santa's been,
 The toys are left as proof.

Rebecca Jackson (11)
Etone Community School

MONDAY MORNING

It's Monday morning and we're always yawning,
I hate that Monday feeling - my mind is reeling.
Homework I've forgotten and there's still things to do,
Oh my God, where's that shoe?

Yes it's Monday morning - the day is dawning.
I hate this early start - the weekend's torn apart.
I've got to get out of bed but I feel like I'm dead.

Michael Dore (13)
Etone Community School

HOMELESS

It rained upon his innocent head,
he would use the park bench for his bed.
All night long he would sit and cry,
under his breath he would softly sigh.

On the corner he would beg for food,
people walk past and think he was being rude.
He walks back down to the park,
all on his own in the dark.

All he wants is to be cared for,
the sorrow he brings would make your heart sore.
Kids walk past and they just laugh,
at this boy sitting on the edge of a path.

Whoever could abandon him,
whoever it was has made a sin.
His clothes could not be worn anymore,
this has to be against the law.

Through the bin he would look,
this poor boy's life someone has took.
One day I wish someone will pray,
that this boy's pain would go away.

Gemma Waring (13)
Etone Community School

WINTER

W e all love wintertime
I wish it could be longer
N ever would it end
T ogether it would be fun
E ndless joy
R ender unto me
S oft and flaky snow

F inally it's winter
L ook at all the snow
A nd all the children
K eep safe
Y ou're wrapped up warm

S ledges are everywhere
N ow it's the end of winter
O h what a shame
W e all love winter.

Mark Williams (11)
Etone Community School

THE FUNKY DUDE

Funky glasses, funky sounds.
Funky walking, funky clowns,
(Smashin' clashin') funky colours.
Funky trouble, funky mothers.

Funky school, funky teacher.
Funky pupil, funky eater.
Funky library, funky books
Funky posters, funky looks.

Funky cafe, funky cups.
Funky coffee, funky gulps.
Funky chairs, funky food.
It's the coolest funky dude.

Rebecca Hibbins (11)
Etone Community School

WASTE LAND

There it sleeps like a huge beast,
With very sharp teeth,
Shaped as metal,
Suddenly it wakes,
And creeps across the brown and green fields.

Huge machines come dumping,
Old tin cans and broken beer bottles,
Old golden cars,
Next to old steel bars,
The pond is green and smelly slime.

On the hill is an old house,
With nickel frames sticking out,
Far away is an old clay factory,
Puffing out filthy grey fumes and stinking gases,
Acid-filled rivers with old beds poking out of the slime.

Every specimen of life is gone,
Killed by the oil - a pollution,
Then the huge beast sleeps,
Waiting . . .

Daniel Fletcher (11)
Etone Community School

CONTINUED

At night when the spirits are near,
you begin to quake and feel very queer;

They come from the alleyways rattling their chains,
down through the lofts and up through the drains;

They carry their weapons sword axe and spear,
the thorny antlers of a roe deer

They hold them up high and bring them down *crash*
onto your bones which splinter and *smash!*

The army of death marches through the night,
who will stand up against their might?

Will good prevail or will it lose?
The choice is here, for you to choose . . .

Thomas Cheffings (13)
Etone Community School

POEM ABOUT MY BEDROOM

M y bedroom is my own special place
Y ou have to knock on the door

B lue is the colour of my carpet and bed
E verywhere posters are hung on the wall
D rawer upon drawer of endless junk
R eading books line up the shelves
O n my desk, my computer sits
O verlooking my black chair
M y room is a place for me.

Neshol Patel (13)
Etone Community School

COULD IT BE?

Could it be,
a big banana,
soaked in silver paint

Could it be,
An unhappy face.
Sad, about something gone wrong,

Could it be,
A happy face
Smiling about a new toy

or

Could it just be, one of God's creations put in that
place to lead us through the dark times?

Nicola Cartwright (13)
Etone Community School

THE LONELY CHILD

I am a loner,
Well that's what the other children call me.
I have no brothers or sisters.
And my father has run away.
My mother is always working.
My only friend is a goldfish,
and all he does is swim around.
I sometimes talk to myself,
Because nobody else likes me.
They call me fatty and smelly,
I hear them laughing at me,
But I don't care.

Mark Styles (13)
Etone Community School

An Acrostic Poem On Birdwatching

B stands for boring which birdwatching really is.
I is for irritating which it is when dad does nothing else.
R stands for rare species which we always have to go and see
(whoopee!)
D is for *driving me up the wall!*
W stands for 'Why do I have to go?'
A is for annoying which it really, really is.
T stands for twitcher (a birdwatcher's real name)
C is for 'Come on or you'll miss it' (shame)
H stands for 'How come it's my dad that does it?'
I is for 'I wish it never had been invented.'
N stands for 'No I am not going thank you!'
G is for 'Go away you stupid birds.'

Chris Smart (13)
Etone Community School

Witch's Spell

Hello and welcome to my dark haunted tree.
This is where I'm going to boil up a treat.
Give me a slimy pea
then add to it a jumping flea.
Give me a can of fizzy Coke
Watch to see if it goes up in a puff of smoke
Wool of bat and tongue of dog
A long wiggly worm and a toe of a frog
The skin of a lion and the tail of a rat
The beak of a bird and the wing of a bat
Blood and bones and some gruesome skin
If it was entered in a competition
Then it would win!

Lisa Hall (13)
Etone Community School

WHO ARE YOU? (A WEST BROMWICH ALBION POEM)

In Alan Miller we've got,
One of the best goalkeepers in the division.
He's 6 foot 3,
And has got great vision.

Our most expensive ever defender is Paul Mardon,
On two occasions he's been on the Welsh international teamlist.
We've also got an Australian called Shaun Murphy,
In 1996 he became an Olympic bronze medalist.

In mid-field there's an Albion fan like me,
He's called Sean Flynn.
We bought him from Derby for £260,000,
And he's determined to win.

On the wing,
There's Kevin Kilbane,
He's an Irish international,
Our record signing, but still a young man.

In attack,
There's Paul Peschisolido,
He's a Canadian international,
And he's better than Savo.

There's also another West Brom fan,
Lee Hughes, who was a non-league star,
But now he's turned professional,
We're all sure he'll go far.

David Evans (13)
Etone Community School

Could It Be Heaven?

Could it be
        the quietest place in the world?
The river flowing so peacefully,
the meadows as green as a Granny Smith apple.

Could it be
        a picture of the world with pieces
of brightly coloured land in the misty lagoon?
With the sky in so many different blends
of azure.

Could it be
        snow-filled orbs in the sky as
pale and unseeing as a blind man's eye?
Could the sky be a mountain? Quiet so
quiet, could it be heaven?

Merrisa Bend (14)
Etone Community School

Spring

As the sun shines and the spring breaks through,
All the memories of me and you,
The happiness that we had together,
Will stay with me forever,
We smelt the freshness of spring,
Listened to the birds sing,
The baby lambs skipped around the field,
The ponies grazed on the hill,
The laughs of the children,
The happiness it makes,
Those were the days of long ago.

Abigail Leadbeater (11)
Etone Community School

THE DEVIL IN ME

She yells and screams,
Whenever she pleases,
She wails and cries and bawls.
She likes nasty dreams,
She hollers and wheezes,
She gets angry and throws things at walls.

She's grumpy and mad,
Never happy, never smiles,
She moans and groans and sulks.
She's nasty and bad.
She winges for miles,
Her mardiness comes in bulk.

She's mad as can be,
She's sad as can be,
She's bad as can be,
That's the devil in me.

Kerry Kendall (14)
Etone Community School

CHOCOLATE

Different shapes and sizes.
Appealing to the eyes,
Packets of multi-colours a rainbow in disguise.
Tickling the tastebuds Crunchie,
Melting pleasing them every one.
From a Fuse to a Galaxy they're all out of this
World.

Kirstie Willis (11)
Etone Community School

Boys

I don't want to disgrace,
The female race,
But I don't get boys these days.

They just stay in bed,
So thick in the head,
I wish they'd smarten up their ways.

They don't brush their hair,
Or wash their face,
And just throw on any old clothes.

I've heard tales,
Of disgusting males,
Are they worth it? Nobody knows.

Gemma Hyde (13)
Etone Community School

My Brother

M y brother is a pain,
Y ou can clearly see he has no brain,

B rothers, I could do without,
R ather have a sister, with no doubt,
O ther than that he's okay,
T hough I would just like to say,
H e does my head in through the day,
E veryone else says he's alright,
R emember he's not your brother all
through the night.

Sarah Garside (13)
Etone Community School

Bonfire Night

Bonfire night,
I love bonfire night with fireworks,
bangers and big bright lights.
Rainbows of colours, sparkling high,
banging and twinkling up to great heights.
Catherine wheels, twisting, whistling around.
Throwing out sparks all around,
to the ground.
Sparklers throw out white sparks make
a hissing sound they're the only thing
that you can hold and shake around.
Fireworks are fun. They make lots of sound.
Bonfire night, bonfire night,
I love bonfire night.

Robert Turner (12)
Etone Community School

Love

Love is a feeling everyone knows,
It makes you tingle from your head to your toes.
You think about them every day,
But you can't tell anyone, anyway.
You walk around with your head in a cloud,
Feeling all flushed and very proud.
Your heart keeps fluttering,
And your mouth keeps stuttering.

Whenever I look up at the moon,
I hope to see my love again soon.

Kiran Grigg (13)
Etone Community School

TAKING MAX FOR A WALK

When I take my dog for a walk,
he runs and runs up the street until
I take him off the lead,
And when I do he just runs across the fields
as if he will never stop,
Then I call him back and throw him another stone,
And off he goes again,
His fur blowing as he runs,
His ears flapping in the wind,
A big smile on his face as he races along,
Then I take him home and he lies down and
goes to sleep.
Until tomorrow when I take him for a walk again.

Lindsey Ridgway (13)
Etone Community School

THE KEY TO THE CASTLE

This is the key to the castle
This is the box
With rusty old lock
That has got the key to the castle

This is the spider thin and small
Who spun his web and sat
And waited
On top of the box
With rusty old lock
That holds the key to the castle.

Nathan Gilliver (12)
Etone Community School

CATS

I have two cats called Ginger and Blax,
They go out at night,
and give mice a fright.
They claw up our carpet,
(and that's how they mark it).
When they were kittens they chewed up my mittens.
When they were young they were really sweet,
we fed them milk and kitten meat.
They're a bit older now,
but they act all the same,
they climb on our furniture,
and mum shouts 'What a pain!'

Nicola Machin (11)
Etone Community School

CAKE

The cakes my grandma makes are very very tasty.
The icing is a creamy white, sticky and a yummy colour.
Sometimes the icing just melts in my mouth.
The icing is very sweet.
That's why I go round nan's for something to eat.
The colour of the sponge is a very hot desert colour
Especially, when they come straight from the oven.
I just stare.
Watching and waiting for a piece to savour!

Claire Rowley (11)
Etone Community School

SISTERS

Sisters. Sometimes they are nice
Sometimes they are awful
But mine is the worst
She thinks she is a Spice Girl
Geri to be precise
She dresses up all spicy
And acts really nice
But when she's not a Spice Girl
She really is naughty.

She hides my books,
She hides my bag,
She hides my pens
And does more things that are bad
But when it's time to sleep
The house is nice and quiet.

She lies in bed,
She sucks her thumb,
She shuts her eyes
And then she's gone.

Ah peace!

Sara Stubbs (11)
Etone Community School

A Space Marine

It stands there plain and undecorated,
I check the box to see what colours are stated.
I grab the paint, I clasp the brush,
Trying ever so hard not to rush.
First the undercoat and when it dries,
I do the little details such as the eyes.
It takes an age, I want it to look good,
Like the one in the shop, like it should.
I persevered through slip and smudge,
The time it took, I didn't begrudge.
For in the end he looked pristine,
My number one blood angel space marine.

The scene is set, the battle's nigh,
I looked my opponent in the eye.
He throws the dice and moves his men,
He throws the dice yet again.
I see his plan I throw the dice,
I move my men not once but twice.
I see a flicker of concern,
His plan, his strategy quite simple to learn.
He sees a mistake in the plan he made,
And he's aware there's a price to be paid.
he counters my move one more time,
'Too late' I say 'victory is mine.'

The joys of victory are not all mine,
I share them with my rank and line.
I dust them off and put them away,
Ready to do battle another day.
But as I close the box did I hear
My blood angel space marines give a cheer?

Sean Crashley (11)
Etone Community School

FEAR FOR A TIGER

I am running,
I cannot stop,
I am out of breath,
but I must breathe.
They are after me, just me.
They want my soft fur, bones and
white teeth.
Bang, off goes a gun
Bullet just touches my fur.
I must run,
get away if I'm to live another day.
Across the deep dark river I swim
They will never get across
The mud's cascading into the water.
I scramble up a bank,
Hooray I'm free.
I will run forever.
I will live on.

Charlotte Courtney (12)
George Eliot School

GOD

Who is he?
Where is he?
What's he look like?
Where's he come from?

Is he true?
Is he just made up?
Is he actually up there?
Is he a big man with a white beard?

What is rain?
What is thunder?
What are all the things that happen?
Does God make it all?

Terri-Marie Lewis (12)
George Eliot School

THE CHURCHYARD

Going through the creaking gates,
I look back at the castle-like walls
surrounding me.
They seem to be pressing in on me
like an army.
It's cold and dark and *scary*

Looking up at the trees,
Their trunks are like old man's
legs striding through the churchyard.
Their branches are outstretching
arms waiting to grab you.
It's cold and dark and *scary*

Bats flying from tree to tree
like trapeze artists.
Big, cold, iron bells clanging like noisy
people all talking at once.
Stone gargoyles staring down at you
like a corpse.
It's cold and dark and *scary.*

Charlotte Lathbury (13)
George Eliot School

THE WIND

Can you see the wind,
Blowing in the trees?
The wind can blow a gale
or can blow a breeze.

Can you hear the wind,
Knocking on the door?
Banging on the window,
I can't stand much more!

Can you feel the wind blowing,
In your face?
Here in a flash,
and gone in a trace.

Can you smell the wind?
Barbecues adrift,
Steak, beefburgers, sausages,
all I swear I whiffed.

Kristine Bradley (12)
George Eliot School

THE RIVER I SEE

As the rain falls into the rainbow-glittered sea of varnish
In admiration I stand mystified at its size
Its strength is that of a giant's
It looks so fragile as fragile as a piece of porcelain
As clear as a continuous pane of glass
Soon the varnish will look as solid as a block of wood
Until then I see another life, it has a life of its own.

Sarah Clarke (12)
George Eliot School

The Wind I See!

As I sit just staring out
watching him move.
He cuts through everything in his path
not caring who or what it is.
He howls like a ravaging wolf
roaming the earth not knowing where to go next.

He's gentle as he helps the sun soften its heat.
He's kind and gentle as well.
He's a helper to the earth
day by day he changes
as he whistles high and low.
By night he roams the coasts and rivers
Making people cold and giving them a chill

He's a person changing his attitude from day to day.

Gemma Goode (12)
George Eliot School

Summer Season

There is a woman in the sky who makes our
summer nice and bright, she makes the sun boil
like tomato soup, which makes the ground as
hot as lava,
She invents ice-cream to cool us down;
She keeps the sky as clear as glass,
I need my sunglasses because the sun is so bright,
and we have a water-fight to cool us down,
We need a drink as cold as ice,
When the sun starts to set we can have a barbecue,
The woman who made summer is a very
summery person.

Meera Rathod (12)
George Eliot School

THE STEALTH

It glides through the air,
Slicing through it like a knife,
It's as silent as an eagle,
Swooping down low.

With bombs in its hold,
And guided by a laser,
This piece of destruction,
Is as deadly as radioactivity.

Suddenly it hits,
Death surrounds it,
Explosions spring up,
The smoke like mushrooms.

Then it's gone,
No one has seen it,
Not even the radars,
Can detect it.

It leaves its mark behind,
To burn away the night,
This multi-million dollar machine,
Is known as . . . 'The Stealth'.

Alex McDonald (12)
George Eliot School

THE SEASONS

Spring warm breeze blow,
girl's gentle smile showed.

Summer sunny days,
anger on her face.

Autumn leaves faded,
upset was expected.

Winter snow fell down.
unhappy was found.

Oi Ka Law (13)
George Eliot School

My Big Brother

My big brother picks on me, tomorrow I'll be in bruises wait and see,
I'm no angel no one is, I'll swap with someone bro for sis.
He plays this game with an egg-shaped ball,
What it's called I've no clue at all.
It's a hard man's game played by women,
I shout to the opposition 'Go on kill 'im'.
He says 'Shut up strange boy or I'll punch you soon.'
I reply, 'Come on then you big baboon.'
After the game we all go home,
And I make fun of this nerdy gnome.
He goes out to work, and comes back at nine,
Chucks me off the computer even though it's mine.
I don't know why, he's got his own,
So I go to his room the danger zone.
Clothes on his chair clothes on the floor,
How many socks lie behind his door?
He walks in and says your room ain't spick and span,
Covered in bruises, you bet I am!
He goes out with his mates, but he won't drink beer,
If it was up to me - he wouldn't be here!

John Quinney (12)
George Eliot School

The Haunted House

The house is haunted,
And very bare.
All the older kids,
Go in, for a scare.

The window shutters,
Are hanging off one hinge.
So when you walk past,
It makes you cringe.

When you see the mess it is a pity,
This scruffy old house in our city.

So pay attention don't buy this house,
Or you might get scared by a squeaky, little
mouse.

Andy Vernon (13)
George Eliot School

Ghosts

When the full moon comes out,
the ghostly ghosts lurk about.
They creep quietly through small cracks,
Behind the doors behind our backs.
Shadow to shadow they creep the wall,
Along with an echoey, echoey call.
The lights go out and the lightning
strikes . . .
And this is what gives me a terrible
fright.

It's a ghost.

Claire Huxley (12)
George Eliot School

Floods

He is a flood that kills people
Destroying everything in his path
He kills all innocent creatures
Cascading through the roads
He swamps all houses
He overflows rivers, feeds on rain
with bodies in his stomach
And water in his throat
There is no escape
From this monster
He is a real killer
Forcing people out of their homes
Then rampaging through all houses
He leaves no rock dry
Everything is under water
He leaves dead people behind him
Destroyed buildings lie wrecked in his path
He leaves many people and creatures homeless
He causes millions in damage
He haunts most people's nightmares
But nobody knows how to stop him
He is known as the
flood.

Scott Friswell (12)
George Eliot School

AUTUMN BRINGS

Leaves swaying like drifting feathers,
Browns, greens, reds all join together like jigsaws,
The sky is bright but colourless,
The sun sparkles through the greyish clouds,
Floating in the misty air one leaf is rotating,

Creatures hiding from their prey,
Drizzling rain is waiting up above,
Multi-colours dashing in your mind.

The glistening sun reaches
through to the wet dew!

Zoe Averns (12)
George Eliot School

DEVIL

D evils going round all night
giving all the kids a fright.

E vil games people play on
this horrible, spooky day.

V arious costumes people wear
to go round and give a scare.

I ndividual people say that
they wish Hallowe'en would go away.

L ittle pumpkins lie around in
every street of every town.

Ellen Phillips (13)
Hartshill School

FRIENDSHIP

Wandering, lonely, watching the other children play,
Standing, quietly, secretly longing for a friend,
Bell goes for the end of break, children rushing,
Giggling, pushing, jostling for position.
While she walks back behind the others,
Still lost without a friend.

Class begins, children chatter amongst themselves,
And sitting alone in the corner, with only her pen
And pencil to accompany her, is the girl.

Her dark skin stands out amongst the bright red
Faces of her classmates,
All oblivious of her presence.
The painful hours of school, slowly tick away
Before eventually the bell goes signalling
The end of her torture.
The girl slowly walks along the road ahead
Still hoping, just hoping, for a friend.

Tom Marshall (14)
Hartshill School

HALLOWE'EN

The stars are so bright,
and I am full of delight
Ghosts and witches,
I am so full of twitches
Brooms are flying
and I am crying.

Louise Owens (12)
Hartshill School

DREAMS

Everyone in this world
Needs their own dream
All dreams can be heard
Up where the clouds are whipped cream.
Dreams are very important
Hope they give to me
Without hope you have nothing
One day you will see.
If you don't have a dream
Then it can't come true
If it did you'd think it's a miracle
But it isn't it's just you.
Whenever you feel sad
The dream you have seems far away
But you will always have hope for it
And keep it day by day.

Kelly Gudger (13)
Hartshill School

WOW, WHAT'S NEW?

Hey Hayley I've got a new body spray
Wow, what's new?
Hayley I've got a new Adidas top
Wow, what's new?
Hayley I've got a new pair of trainers
Wow, what's new?
Hayley I've got a new CD
Wow, what's new? But have you ever thought
About giving up bragging?

Hayley Biddle (12)
Hartshill School

Animal

Rabbits, hamsters, dogs and cats
Snakes, lizards, mice and rats
All these we have as pets
When catching fish you need a net
People have loads of pets
When they die you get upset
The vets did everything they could
The owners thought the vet was good
Buy a new one
Call it Tom
Have lots of fun
And get housework done
Tom the budgie starts to fly
And your cat curled up to die
Then you get upset again
Tom flies off and it starts to rain.

Lindsay Hall (13)
Hartshill School

The UFO

The lights were shining on the field that night.
I looked at the sky and saw a disc.
It landed about two yards in front of me
I looked a lot closer and saw a silvery shadow.
It began to rain, that night the moon was shining.
The figure came close and spoke.
'Blub blub up a do.' I was scared, then it tried
to kill me. I ran into the woods that night.
I'll never forget that night.

Graeme Gudger (12)
Hartshill School

TRICK OR TREAT

Little children going out guess what it's
Hallowe'en night!
Knocking on doors, trick or treat.
Stamping of little kids' feet.
Hallowe'en.
11 Kipling Close, creaking floors.
Knock on the door
In you go, woo
On the floor a dead man
Ahh!
A ghost
Trick or treat.

Cheryl Fox (12)
Hartshill School

JULILLY'S FEAR

I'm sad and powerless
I have been dragged from Mammy Sally.
Everything I had has been taken,
Like candy being taken from a baby.
My throat is dry.
I'm alone and horrified.
I hope I wake up now and it's been all a dream.
I miss Mammy Sally and our cabin with the
polished floor.
I feel like I've been used,
Like an old rag and thrown away.

Amy Jayne Matts (12)
Hartshill School

HALLOWE'EN

Hallowe'en is a time of year
When little children have big fears
Goblins dancing, laughing evil
Leave the door as they are meanful
Little kids lighting candles
Watch it they might grab your door handle
Hallowe'en is kind of spooky
Witches' spells send you loopy
Watch it now and don't allow
The black cat it screams miaow
Hallowe'en is in the midnight hour
Give them a treat, egg and flour
Now in Dover
Hallowe'en is over
So lock your doors
And block your drive
As next year, they will be back alive.

Aaron Sheridan (13)
Hartshill School

RUNNER BEAN

They call me runner
That's a lie, though I wish I could
I'm stuck on a breadboard
And about to be chopped
I'll soon be cooked and eaten
What shall I do?
I can feel the steel blade
Pressing harder harder harder.

Adam Brown (12)
Hartshill School

I'M JUST LIKE YOU!

People stare and walk away,
Whenever I come near,
It's true that no one likes me,
That's pretty clear.

But why do they whisper about me,
And write notes about me too,
I want to be like other children,
Just the same as you.

Because I've got a disability,
Doesn't mean I have to be ignored,
I start to think about myself,
Whenever I get bored.

Everyone stops and stares,
When I come outside to play,
I go and sit in my corner,
Then everyone turns away.

Why is it that no one likes me,
Why do they stare,
Maybe they think I'm a mean monster,
Stuck in a wheelchair.

I know I'm not the same as you,
I know I can't do the same things as you,
But I am a human being,
Please, just once, couldn't you treat me like
Other people too?

Kate Marshall (11)
Hartshill School

The Black Moon!

Deep in the midnight moon,
Out come witches on their brooms.
People going around in different faces,
Wandering around in different places.

Bonfires, fireworks flaming high,
Reaching and screeching to the sky.

The sky is blue,
The grass is green.
A penny or two for,
Hallowe'en!

Trick or treat,
A penny or a sweet.
Saying that to everyone,
Who they meet.

Deep in the midnight moon,
Out come witches on their brooms.
People going around in different faces,
Wandering around in different places.

Darren Brown (14)
Hartshill School

A Poem About Life

Life is for living helping and giving
Some people like taking and hassle just making
They don't think of others when mess they are making
They don't think of the stress they are creating
If people thought more of the helping and giving
What better *life* we could all have.

Samuel Hands (12)
Hartshill School

Hallowe'en Party

Everybody rushes to the party on Hallowe'en,
All trying their best to scream.
They all run down the street,
All they want is a bite to eat.
The house stands out from half a mile,
Everyone's acting like it's a big crocodile.
They all rush in,
And fall over the bin.
A girl got bit on the knee,
By a big green flea.
She thought she would die,
Everyone laughed and said it's only a fly,
As if you are going to die.
The music got turned off,
All because it disturbed a moth.
That was the end of the night,
And off went the light.

Louise Brown (12)
Hartshill School

Hallowe'en

It's time to trick or treat,
all the costumes are nice and neat.
Watch the ghosts come out to play,
believe it won't make your day.
Devils come out at midnight,
make sure you turn off the light.
The mummy stomps around,
with a gun.
So you'd better *run!*

Kevin Jones (13)
Hartshill School

The Pumpkin

People in the streets below
Under supervision
More and more keep coming
And knocking on the door.

Pumpkins at the door giving
Everyone a scare
Kiddies all dressed up in costumes
Like witches, ghosts and ghouls.

Innocent faces when they say
Trick or treat penny or sweet
Now Hallowe'en is over people are
Going home to eat their sweets
And count their money.

Emma Elverson (13)
Hartshill School

Hallowe'en

The clock strikes 12 the ghosts come out,
Witches and vampires are lurking about.
It's the 31st October, it's Hallowe'en,
When ghosts and ghouls are really mean.
Ghosts never, ever come out in the day,
When it is nice and sunny.
They only ever come out at night,
And steal your sweets and money.
Watch out for broomsticks in the sky,
While you're not watching they might fly by.
So watch out when this time of year comes by,
Hold on to your beds or you might die.

Gemma McLeod (13)
Hartshill School

HALLOWE'EN

H allowe'en, Hallowe'en witches,
ghosts and devils

A udiences are gathering in
the street they are waiting for
the witching hour and for
the witches to appear.

L ittle boys dress as devils
little rebels

L ittle girls dress as witches
take their brooms and
they're in stitches.

O ctober is the month the
31st is the day.

W itches huddle around
cauldrons to make spells
to turn kids into toads then
you hear yells.

E veryone is getting ready
to trick or treat to get
little sweets.

E very witch, every ghost is
getting ready to spook.

N ever go out on Hallowe'en
night if you don't want a
fright.

Kerry Hamilton (13)
Hartshill School

DEVILS

D evils round the darkest night
seeking children to give a fright

E ndless terror down in hell
so close your eyes and cast a spell

V ictorious devils seize the world
the witch's cauldron has been swirled

I ntended pain on empty souls,
human hearts in breakfast bowls

L ots of blood ready and cold
for the vampires have been told

S pells are cast they are the worst
for October the 31st.

Scott Osborne (14)
Hartshill School

HALLOWE'EN

Tonight's the night
We come to play,

Trick or treat is the
Way we play,

Wicked witches,
Deadly devils,
Glaring ghosts,

So don't go out or
You'll be in for a
Fright.

Carl Hutchison (12)
Hartshill School

HALLOWE'EN

H owling ghosts in the
graveyard.

A ll the bats' eyes, frogs' legs
and spiders all in one big
black cauldron.

L ittle children afraid of the
night.

L augh no more.

O wls squawking what a
fright.

W icked witches fly through
the night.

E veryone is there to
scare.

E eks and screams everywhere.

N ow remember never say trick
or treat, it could be you
the witches eat!

James Barr (12)
Hartshill School

SCARY

S hivering down the street at night
C atching ghost but hit lamppost
A nd children under spells
R un run from the witch's wells
Y ahhh as they run run run.

Colin Straker (13)
Hartshill School

A Picked Rose

Julilly, only a budding flower,
Taken,
Taken from her forgotten rose bush,
At the bottom of her forgotten garden.

Picked from her bush,
From her garden,
Tossed aside,
Alone.

A lonely rose head,
Crumpled and empty,
The feeling of injustice overwhelmed her,
She misses the others of her rose bush.

Her thorns too small to do any damage to anyone,
Her petals shall never open.
To the friendly outside world,
Julilly, only a budding flower.

Leigh Stallard (12)
Hartshill School

Hallowe'en

When all is dark on Hallowe'en night
All of evil comes to life
With cauldrons churning
And pumpkins burning
And witches casting their spells
But when the ghost comes out to play
Do you dare to stay up late
And all is well on Hallowe'en
But the question is do you believe?

Janine Turvey (13)
Hartshill School

JULILLY

Julilly was frightened,
She had nobody to depend on,
She was alone, scared and helpless
She was in need of a friend.
Her mouth was as dry as a desert
landscape.
She was depressed and unhappy,
She needed water nearly as much as
she needed Mammy Sally.
She would be whipped to death
if she disobeyed her master.
Her heart was empty without
Mammy Sally,
She could do well as a slave
if she could be bothered but it was
hopeless, she felt used and suicidal.

Charlotte Brindley (13)
Hartshill School

SPELL FOR A WITCH

After twelve the witches begin their spell
it kinda goes like this.
Finger nail of a horse
rabbit's tail even better
Plus don't forget the most important ingredient
a little brat about 4 feet tall.
Turn it round and hear it *pop* then serve it
up for dinner
After eating it all you'll look younger and
graceful again.

Jennifer Bucknall (13)
Hartshill School

PONY

Bye my lovely pony
I'll miss you such a lot
It makes me cry when I say goodbye
And I think of your favourite spot

I'll soon buy another pony
I'll name it after you
I'll clean it out and put it out
In the field that I put you in too

I'll take it out for a ride
I'll visit you each day
I'll bring him down
I'll make him sound
So you both can go and play.

Elaine Brown (12)
Hartshill School

SMOKE

The way they just stand around,
Not caring who's about,
All those innocent victims,
Cancer's struck them down.
The smoky air,
The stagnant smell,
The people won't declare,
For they know as well as we do,
The end's not far from now.

Kate Brown (12)
Hartshill School

SCHOOL

Don't
you think
it's really unfair
when teachers do
things to give you a
scare
And when you get
sent outside in the
wind, sleet or snow
and the teachers sit
in the staff room just
telling boring jokes.
But the music lessons
are the worst 'cause
you get made to
sing
and you just sit praying
for the bell to
ring!

Janine Turvey (13)
Hartshill School

HER FEELINGS

She felt devastated
She was badly treated
Her eyes were as red as a rose
She felt alone without her mom
The tears ran down her face
She needed a friend
All she could think of was home.

Ryan Stuart Ashby (12)
Hartshill School

FRIENDSHIP

Lonely hearts begin to solve,
the mystery of lasting friendship.
Strong feelings of their presence,
begin to fade within time.
Secrets shared,
a shoulder to cry upon.
The world seemed to have no
boundaries,
for our common sense was needed.
We were like peas in a pod,
forever together.
After all a day without a smile,
is a wasted day.
Laughter was our motto,
for each and every day.
She was a memory to gaze upon,
when we were apart.
I always know,
she will be in my heart.

Natalie Osadciw (13)
Hartshill School

HALLOWE'EN

Hallowe'en is scaring to death
Scary faces in the cold dark night
Children crying because they are scared
Ghosts watching everywhere
People saying 'Trick or treat' in the dull night
Witches say 'Double double toil and trouble'
To make people scared
Hallowe'en everywhere.

Tanneke De Vogel (13)
Hartshill School

Hallowe'en

H allways creaking with the
walking ghosts

A round the streets kids are
trick or treating

L oud laughing of
werewolves

L oving pumpkin in the
window

O wls hooting in the
trees

W itches flying high up
in the sky

E verything allows the witch
to take over

E verything stops for the
witch

N one is moving in case
the witch casts a spell.

Mathew Stanley (12)
Hartshill School

The Blob!

The blob comes out on Hallowe'en
Looking for little kids to eat
For tea he comes from the woods
Far away no one dares go outside
Everyone is scared of the blob.

No one can see him
Because he blends in with the bushes.
The blob started off a little thing
And then got bigger eating everything.

Daren Eggleton (12)
Hartshill School

Carry On Winning!

James through to Jones,
Straight down the side,
Passes to Ince,
The fans feel pride.

Ince through to Murphy,
The new super red,
Decides to chip it,
Over Pallister's head.

Leonhardson collects the ball,
Long pass to Bjornebye,
All the supporters think,
Is this really going to be?

Bjornebye crosses to Fowler,
Oh, it's hit the bar!
But out it comes to Riedle,
He's a superstar!

He takes it round Beckham,
As United stand in awe,
As Riedle gives it to McManaman,
Who adds one more.

Sammy Lee (13)
Hartshill School

Skeletons

S keletons with their wretched bones, hang about to touch their toes,
with no skin but all with bones, with no flesh but all with toes.
K illing all those little brats, who kick and scream from the rats,
who will soon become bats.
E very little brat around will soon be on the ground, with their mouths
open wide screaming to stay alive.
L ittle children with tears in their eyes, crying out to the skies,
praying with their tearful fears hoping the ghost won't come near.
E very kid around, will no longer make a sound, but all the ghouls
with all their tools could give you a little fright.
T he twinkle in the devil's eye, could be a sign to say goodbye,
or you will have a big fry or maybe die.
O nward go the little brats, knock, knock while standing on the mat
waiting for a trap which might not even be a bat.
N obody will ever stare, at that awful witch's hair, if they want to
stay alive, they'll stay well away from the drive .
S creaming while the witches fly, onwards in the deep blue sky,
while all of the bats go by.

Rachael Beardall (13)
Hartshill School

Witches

It was Hallowe'en night
ghosts, ghouls, witches
and skulls come out of
their coffins and
scare
scare
scare.

James Percival (12)
Hartshill School

LOVE IN HEAVEN

Sad is a thing I feel,
A home is a thing I had,
A crime is what has happened,
Terrified is what I am.

Hurt is what we all are,
Tears are in the wind,
And freedom in the soul.

Heaven is the land of dreams,
But still so far away,
Love was all around us,
But now it's hidden away.

Charlotte Ann Croft (12)
Hartshill School

HALLOWE'EN

T rick, egg and flour
R un the devil's coming
I cky sticky goo
C old water falling on you
K icking cabbages

Or

T reats, I want sweets
R efresher bars we would like
E ndless treats all through the night
A nts screaming for all sorts
T reats is what we want.

Michael Elkin (13)
Hartshill School

Hallowe'en

Hallowe'en comes once a year,
Bringing loads of fearsome fear.

Laughing witches getting ready to
Doom,
It's coming to us very soon.

Get ready and lock your door,
Because the vampires are coming
To explore.

All the kiddies are having a
Fright,
Because the horrors of Hallowe'en
Are coming to *bite*.

Jade Paintin (14)
Hartshill School

Horses

Horses walking this way and that,
A pony there he's in a trap.

I love foals and ponies too,
That pony's numnah's the colour blue.

Galloping, cantering a halt then a jump,
After we trotted over a bump.

We galloped back to the stables,
Our ride had ended for the day.

Joanne Short (12)
Hartshill School

Julilly's Feelings

Julilly was feeling 'done over',
She felt as though she was being used.
She couldn't sleep without Mammy Sally
there to comfort her.
The cart jumped about throwing Julilly
and the other kids across the cart.
She bounced along feeling that the world
was coming to an end, she was depressed.
The tears suddenly flowed out like a rushing
stream, she was distraught.
She gave Willy's hand a little squeeze
still deep in thought.
Little Willy started to moan, Julilly
comforted him.
Julilly was on her way to Mississippi
'The Deep South'.

Lorna Tarplin (12)
Hartshill School

School Is So Boring

'School is so boring' someone said one day,
So why don't we all go away.
'I have had a boring day today' someone said that day,
It's home time now hip, hip, hooray.
We re going to Summer Bay today,
By the beach and far away.
We played sand castles one hot day,
Now it's time to go bye, bye.

Lucy Carne (12)
Hartshill School

JULILLY'S RIDE

Into the cart like useless meat
Down the road was all so quiet
Nobody around feeling abandoned.
Sad, frightened, lonely, scared
Seeing people ploughing fields.

Mammy Sally where are you?
I'm so upset so please help me
The clouds in the sky,
So like cotton buds
I am alone and very thirsty.

I'm so angry that I can't see you
I'm so confused and so mad
I feel like dirt,
Dirty, unclean and so unhealthy
I hope I'll make the journey today
I'll need a rest and then a play.

Melissa Day (12)
Hartshill School

JULILLY

Julilly was as scared as a wild rabbit
that had been captured,
The younger children that sobbed beside
her reminded her of how much she
would miss Mammy Sally.
She felt as if she was alone in the world,
She was as thirsty as a working camel in
the desert,
She had been down-graded.

Nicola Ashtiaq (12)
Hartshill School

STARS

Stars are in the sky
Shining bright with the moon
The planets are there too
It will be light soon.

The night is dark
The moon is full
Groups of stars around
There are some in the shape of a bull.

There is a group called Orion
With a dog by his side
You can also see the North Star
It can take a while to find.

You can also get shooting stars
That fly through the sky at speed
They may be heading for Mars
But I can't see the need.

Helen Holt (13)
Hartshill School

WINTER

Winter! I love it.
I love the glistening snow,
making footsteps, sledding,
snowballs and snowmen.

Freezing fingers,
tingling face, nose aglow,
days of fun and hours of play.
Winter! I love it.

James Rathbone (12)
Hartshill School

Voodoo Voodoo

Little voodoo doll sat over there
You can't look at it
So powerful its stare

Evil so strong pulsing
With a hypnotic beat
Waiting for victims
To lay at the devil's own feet

This is a doll
Above other dolls
Waiting to tempt
Weak and vengeful souls

Someone sat with the doll
Vengeful glee making them stab
Cruel as a cat with twice the spite
How would they like it if they got a jab

So small, so small
A doll above dolls
Filled with black magic
Torturing souls

Don't go near
It will capture your soul
This forever evil doll

Eyes that are staring
Eyes that are glaring
Filled with vengeful pleasure
That no devil could measure

This voodoo doll
Has lasted through time
How we should wish
It had been left behind.

Juliet Reeves-Eastwood (14)
Hartshill School

JULILLY'S FEELINGS

The days are so lonely,
and long without my Mammy Sally.
We desperately need to escape.
I'm hungry, but I don't feel like eating,
because I'm too sad and angry.
I feel so destroyed inside,
and that something
has been taken away from me.
I really hate it
when they tie me up,
because I feel like an animal,
not a human.
My tears flow like a waterfall
that never ever stops.
I'm petrified and confused,
of what they might do next,
but I just have to keep on working,
I really can't wait to see her again,
if I ever do,
so we can plan a route to get out of this
horrible place and to Canada.

Nicola Hadley (12)
Hartshill School

The Journey That Seemed To Be The End

Slung into the wagon like worthless animals,
Down the dusty cobbled road,
Lonely, petrified, empty, hurt.
My heart sank as we were led away.

The rocky wagon turned a corner,
Fear buzzing around our heads like a trapped, angry bee,
Tears trickled down my rounded face like a slow, steady, stream
It was hopeless, my past life and memories were being snatched away.

Young children in the wagon had given up and whimpered.
I swallowed a long hard swallow,
The sour taste of the fat man's fingers still in my mouth.
My throat was dry, my stomach was empty.

Round another twisted road,
Where were we?
Where were we going,
Who knew?
Blankness and loneliness filled our heads like a book
with only one letter inside.

Emma Ashby (12)
Hartshill School

First Day At School

First day at school. I wake up and I did not
want to go to school.
It was really gruesome, I got in the
car and drove to school and went
round to the playground. The bell went
and I went in the hall to have an
assembly.

Adam Robinson (11)
Hartshill School

Hallowe'en

H allowe'en, Hallowe'en who believes in
Hallowe'en?
A ll lanterns gleaming, different people
screaming.
L ong screams and funny things.

L ong nights all with frights.

O pening the door, hearing trick or treat,
I just give you a little sweet.

W ind howling people growling.

E vil witches fooling, with little children
ruling.

E ating pumpkin all with something.

N ew spells with many yells.

Victoria Ward (13)
Hartshill School

My School

The teachers are really cool
the dinners are ace
the school is massive
and there's lots of children
most are football mad
spelling sucks
maths is cool
but most of all *hometime* is the coolest
of it all.

Scott McEwan (11)
Hartshill School

ANNE FRANK'S DIARY

I'm horrified
I feel trapped
There's no food here
I'm feeling hungry
I'm crying
I'm upset
Hitler's trapped me
I feel sick
I want to go home
There's no water
I'm thirsty
I'm tired
I'm dirty
It's frustrating
It's smelly
I'm scared too
I'm really homesick.

Nicole Cleave (11)
Hartshill School

THE DISCREET

All Hallows Eve in the dead of night,
There lies a creature to give a fright.
He controls this world but he isn't a god,
The mind he owns, your eyes his own.
This is the creature you cannot defeat,
He kills off animals till they're extinct,
And wrecks the land and is very discreet.
Quite a while of this beast I do speak,
People are the monster which you do seek.

Christopher Martin (15)
Hartshill School

ANNE'S DIARY

Dear Kitty,

My stomach churned
as I walked through
the big iron gates
of the concentration
camp. I'm tired and
upset and I want to
go home I'm trapped
and can't escape. I
feel lifeless and need
help. I'm frustrated and
hungry too. I also need
the loo. I'm petrified
here in the dark, I
pray to God every day
that the fear will
go away.

Bye bye Kitty.

Rebecca Campbell (11)
Hartshill School

SPIDERS

S pitting venom around the place
P acing up and down your face
I n your flesh you feel their fangs
D eadly spiders attack in gangs
E nds your life with a tiny nip
R ip your skin tear and strip
S piders are watching you!

Elliot Caddy (13)
Hartshill School

HOMELESS

When the cold wind chills you,
Chills you to the bone.
You've got no money,
And you're sitting all alone.

Down in deep dark alleyways,
In corner shop doors.
Begging for money,
It's for a good cause.

You have your sturdy sleeping bag,
And your rucksack too.
The rain comes down and hits your face,
And your clothes are soaked right through.

The passers-by just look at you,
Then they walk away.
You have this dream inside your mind,
You'll be like them some day.

Alison Aucott (13)
Hartshill School

PUMPKINS

P eople with pale faces
U gly masks and ugly costumes
M ad adults - sick of children knocking
P eople carrying pumpkins
K nock, knock, 'Trick or treat?'
I mpatient children.
N oisy little kids
S pooky sounds being made.

Jenna Haldane (12)
Hartshill School

Hitler

I'm scared,
Hitler,
I'm hungry,
Hitler,
I'm dirty,
Hitler,
I'm crying,
Hitler,
I'm ready for death,
Hitler,
There's no food,
Hitler,
Hitler I hate you,
Why do you go after us?

Emily Arkinstall (11)
Hartshill School

My Two And A Half Weeks At Hartshill

When I came to Hartshill school,
Mr Morgan was so cool,
I love the smell of the dinners,
I'm not scared of the year elevens,
I'm not even scared of Mr West,
I will live in the uniform,
I'm so nervous of getting told off,
Not bringing my homework in,
Being late for lessons,
I hope I don't get pushed down the stairs,
I see all of my friends.

Emma Harris (11)
Hartshill School

WAR IN IRELAND

There's a war raging
Why?
Another heart's breaking
Why?
Another gun's firing
People running, people hiding
But why?
Twenty foot perimeter walls
Soldiers, lots of them, bombing schools
Why would someone do that?
No one wants to
They're all forced to
Who forces them?
If you kill someone,
You needn't be afraid of them . . .

Zac Davies (13)
Hartshill School

THE ANNE FRANK EXPERIENCE

I hate this place!
It's a real disgrace,
This concentration camp,
Is smelly and damp.
People are tortured every day,
Then they're killed in a horrid way.
People are beaten with planks of wood,
And can we escape? Oh I wish we could.
This is horrid. Oh me! Oh my!
I can hear a child cry and cry.
This small cold room gives me chills,
While Hitler's gas room kills and kills.

Sam Essex (11)
Hartshill School

IN A HOSTEL HOME

Dear Monty,

I'm no better, I'm scared, terrified
and cold.
I don't know where my dad is,
We are all upset and we can't
see each other because we are
in a little dark room.
I haven't had anything to eat
because all that's been on the menu
was a sip of water and dried oats.
I've heard that families are being split
up and being gassed and shot and
then being put in a big pit with
thousands more dead people.
I hope I don't get gassed or shot
because that would be the end
of a very short worthless life.

James Everard (11)
Hartshill School

THE END OF ANNE FRANK

It was the last day of being alive
Before they put me in the gas room.
I wish they would kill me today so it would be all over.
I am so scared I am shaking so much.
I miss my family too much.
I wish it was a dream and I would wake up and see my
family and say I had a really awful dream.
I don't want to *die.*

Natasha Perkins (11)
Hartshill School

The Doll Of Sticks

He stares at me like the devil's eyes,
He looks like a spider dressed in disguise,
His arms are as rough as the bark on a tree,
The voodoo doll is looking for me.

As I walk along the corridor,
Creep, creep goes the creepy old floor,
Petrified as I walk down the staircase,
Isn't this a freaky old place.

A skeleton of sticks all in a bundle,
Making the sound of a burble,
Scared and suspicious,
Torture and pain,
I will never come here to see the
Voodoo doll again.

Aimee Oakley (14)
Hartshill School

The Awful End Of Anne Frank

It's terrifying in a small room,
I am really lonely.
It is horrifying.
I knew I was going to die, because I was already
tired and shaky.
I am hungry and thirsty, ready to get up and
scream, but I couldn't.
It was awful.
I wish I was still at home, with my family.
It would be much better than this.
It wouldn't be so smelly and dirty.
I would rather be dead than suffer in here.

Sarah Morris (12)
Hartshill School

IMPRISONED

I was lying under the car fixing the device to the engine,
I heard someone get into the car, the device was set.
I put on my Balaclava and slid away. I got up and began to run,
The bomb went off. I fell to the floor in pain.
The family in the car were dead. I couldn't move.
Whether it was out of pain or shock, I don't know.
I finally got up and began to run.
Too late to look back, I ran to the park.
The van was parked by the playground,
I saw a flash it was destroyed and flaming.
I had no escape, angry locals behind, Protestants to my right,
The van in front and police to my left.
I ran to the police and turned myself in.
The hammer came down, I had to face fifteen years.

Matthew Potter (14)
Hartshill School

MY ANNE FRANK POEM

I was so terrified and dirty that I was ready for death,
so I felt very upset that I am going to leave my mom.
Of course my father was dead so I was horrified.
All of a sudden a big bang went off.
I was hungry and I felt that I was trapped,
and I could not move because I was frightened.
My mom came to me and gave me something to eat,
and I was so sick I stank like my sick,
and of course I could not have a bath,
then a bomb landed on my house and made a big bang,
and I was hurt, and scared.

Dean Pate (11)
Hartshill School

THE BOMB!

All of a sudden there she was,
My sister, lying in the road
The bomb had gone off suddenly,
Nobody knew what was happening
People rushing around trying to help
I went over to her
Blood was pouring out of her leg
like water out of a tap.
I was shouted at 'Help her then!
Go on help her'
But all I could do was stand there
shocked by what had happened
Bang!
Another bomb gone off just down
the road
I didn't care, all I could think about
was my sister.

Kirsty Miles (13)
Hartshill School

UNCLE JAMES

My uncle James was a terrible man,
He cooked his wife in a frying pan,
She's so tender to bake or boil,
He fried her up in cooking oil.
But some time later at my uncle's door,
A great green devil was standing there,
He grabbed my uncle by the hair,
Oh never more oh never more
There will be a knock at my uncle's door.

Luke Beardmore (12)
Hartshill School

The Sound Of War

A gunshot.
Like a shriek from a hundred dying people.
With my heart in my throat,
I had to keep running,
I had to escape,
I had to do what I did.
I wouldn't have done it if it wasn't for them.
I had to run,
I had to climb,
I had to jump,
The IRA have hearts made of stone.
The guns again.
Won't they ever stop,
Will there ever be peace?

Rebecca Lewis (13)
Hartshill School

The Voodoo That Youdoo

Black like an alley cat
Vengeful as a poison rat.
Wandering round it's looking for me
It changes shape like an autumn tree.
Stranger than the darkest night
This kind of doll will give you a fright.
The power voodoo dolls have inside
It's kind of like a scary ride.
So whether voodoo's true or not
It's strange just like a winter that's
hot.

Kevin Mullins (14)
Hartshill School

WHY ME?

I was running,
I was running as if there were a thousand
elephants behind me.
All I could hear were bombs going off.
I'd look behind me,
No one was there.
My thoughts were racing,
Would I live to see another day?
Maybe I would wake up soon,
Or Mother would tell me to snap out
of it.
It was like I was having a nightmare,
But I knew this was no dream,
It was reality,
And they were after *me!*

Laura Stringer (13)
Hartshill School

WHO CAN DO VOODOO?

Eyes looking through me like stone
Unflinching cutting through all my thoughts
Like a knife through butter
Thinking of black magic
An old woman starts to mutter
Ooo voo doo
Death
Spirits aroused
Then bang it's all gone
The woman disappears
The route of all fears.

Kent W Dwyer (14)
Hartshill School

The Witch's Verse

Double double toil and trouble
Fire burn and cauldron bubble
Fillet of snake in the cauldron boil to bake
Eye of frog and toe of newt
Woof of dog and tongue of bat
Adder's fork and blind worm's sting
Lizard's leg and butterfly wing
For a charm of powerful
Trouble like a hell broth boil
And bubble
Double double toil and trouble
Fire burn and cauldron bubble.
In a turn of firesome trouble
Let the cauldron scream and bubble.

Katie Brookes (12)
Hartshill School

Mystery Doll

Its eyes of spite
Just staring at me
I can feel the black magic
Capturing my soul
The mysterious unsolved
But yet I can feel
The anger and vengefulness
The ugly fearful thing feels
Against me.

Claire Doughty (14)
Hartshill School

PEACEFUL WALK

I was walking along the battered pavement
Trying not to step on the cracks.
It was a lovely sunny day with a cool breeze . . .
I heard footsteps behind me it was a gang of
Youths, they passed peacefully.
I looked up at the sky a white dove was
Flying joyfully through the blue sky.
I slowed down and turned into the shop.
I bought some flour because my mum
Wanted to bake a birthday cake for my sister.
I walked out of the shop and
Back onto the battered pavement.
Bang! It went like an earthquake.
The gentle breeze turned into a blast
And the blue sky turned black,
And the white flour went up in the air . . .
As the dove came floating down.

Louise Chérif (14)
Hartshill School

VOODOO DOLL

Voodoo doll you are the scariest,
Voodoo doll you are the hairiest,
Even though you are so small, you could be so very cruel.
Your eyes stare into mine, as I stand there so petrified,
You could be as destructive as a bulldozer,
Even though you are as light as a feather.
Get me away from here, but most of all away from the fear.

Jonathan Young (14)
Hartshill School

ON THE TRAIN

I was on the train
People were shouting and crying
I was sitting with my family
Having probably the last laugh
When the train stopped
Men got on and dragged people off
Strongish people including my Dad
Some got away
Then we got told to get off
I think I will be killed tonight
We dug a grave
Then we had some bread
My family passed away.

James Ritchie (11)
Hartshill School

VOODOO DOLL

Voodoo doll you are *dead* cool,
Even though you are so cruel,
You are scary as well as hairy,
You look so queer you fill me
with fear,
With a pin in your head you
smell like a donkey cart,
You look so sad you must be bad,
Eyes as black as coal you look
like a troll,
Covered in cloth as silent as a
moth.

Terry Paul (14)
Hartshill School

MUM AND ME

Mum and me are together in everything we do,
But when it comes to a question
We haven't got a clue,
We'll be best friends forever, and
Never will that fade,
But soon we will separate
When we come the age.
Mum says I'm her darling,
I say she's my chum,
And when we have an argument,
We're sorry for what we've done.
When my mum is mad I keep well away
And when she calms down a bit,
I say ho ha, ho ha.
As I said earlier,
We're best friends forever and never
Will that fade,
And when we die we'll know for
Sure we'll be in the same *graves.*

Laura Ashby (11)
Hartshill School

VOODOO DOLL

Eyes as dark and glaring as night
And decorations as bright as the sun.
It's a mixture of all the good and bad
things that you've ever done.
So small and brittle and will amuse
This voodoo doll you will never dare
use.

Matthew Glover (14)
Hartshill School

Football, Football The Beautiful Game

I watch it in the sun, and I watch it in the rain.
Football, football the beautiful game.
My favourite commentator Andy Gray,
Tells us how the players play.

I think that Cov play very very lame.
Football, football the beautiful game.
Man U are top. Man U are the best.
Much, much better than all the rest.

Footballers these days get all the fame.
Football, football the beautiful game.
There's a goal here, there's a goal there.
The players get their shirts from Mothercare.

Football, football the beautiful rain.
Off goes the water and on comes the game.
Keane and Ince are in a lot of pain.
Football, football the beautiful game.

Neil Percival (12)
Hartshill School

Voodoo Doll

It is like a small evil bird,
Its eyes are like black coals,
I feel like a rabbit in a trap,
Caught up in all the anger and hate,
It is as if I am being stalked,
Everywhere I turn it is there,
Making sure I can't get away,
I'll never get away,
After all no one escapes from a voodoo doll.

Samantha Swami (14)
Hartshill School

Daffodils Are Aliens!

Daffodils are aliens,
They come from outer space.
They were meant to go to Zog world,
But they came to the wrong place.

They came here in a spaceship,
And sank into a bog.
They're growing here instead of,
On the planet Zog.

With guns and lasers
And secret powers,
And even flying saucers,
But still you call them flowers.

Daffodils or flowers,
Call them what you wish.
But that's not what they're really called,
'Cos they've been named Zogish.

So don't go near the meadows,
Nor near the rivers.
'Cos once you've seen a Zogish,
You'll always have the shivers!

Kelly Greenaway (11)
Hartshill School

The Last-Minute Goal

Newcastle and Man U playing the game.
Here come Newcastle on the run again.
Shearer to Howey, Howey to Lee.
The ball's in the net and they all go ape.

The score's one all the last seconds of the game.
The crowd's all silent once again.
The ball's with Albert he doesn't look up.
He lobs Peter Schmeichel and he wins the Cup.

Lee Straker (12)
Hartshill School

HELP!

Underneath the water
Going down and down
I can't swim to the surface
I just know I'm going to drown

I need some help
I need some air
I see a flicker
Of light up there

The flicker is coming closer
I can see an awful shape
It's got a big fat belly
It just looks like an ape

It seems to be touching me
It's kind of picking me up
It's holding on to me
But we seem to be going up

It's just all gone black
For one split second,
There's a man lying next to me
And I think I've just awakened.

Nikki Owen (12)
Hartshill School

AUTUMN

The air gets cold
the leaves fall down
the ground is covered
orange and brown

The wind gets up
there's frost on the ground
the leaves are swirling
round and round

The trees are bare
the leaves are scattered around
there's many colours
covering the ground

It's nearly winter
it's even worse
but then it will be spring
and the ice will disperse.

Jamie Steggles & Richard Gazeley (11)
Hartshill School

WITCH

W icked witch
I n the wicked cupboard witches fly
T error with wicked witches
C ats all in black
H orror in the night.

Matthew Sears (13)
Hartshill School

Rainforest Destruction

We used to live in peace and harmony
With the living trees
Until one day greedy men decided
They wanted more farmland by
Rainforest destruction.

They chopped down the trees we need
The trees we need for air
These people that are chopping
Down our trees do not seem to care.

They do not seem to understand how
Much we need our rainforest
They want it for farms
And roads, doesn't anyone care anymore?

Nobody understands our way of life anymore
Why does nobody care about our trees?
We need so much,
One day they too will die because
Of rainforest destruction.

Vicky Whopples (11)
Hartshill School

Wicked Witches

W icked witches
I njured cats
T error witches
C ats' eyes
H allowe'en

Gemma Morton & Bernadette Arnold (13)
Hartshill School

Why Me?

My friends and I were playing one day,
Running around like a hamster in a wheel,
The cool breeze whistling through our hair,
Then the sky went grey, and we were covered in cloud,
The cool breeze turned to a gale-force wind,
It was as though some kind of evil was about,
Two of my friends staggered back, staring at me,
I wondered what they were doing,
Then, I went cold,
I was frozen to the spot,
I felt a cold, hard blade on my spine,
Blood carpeted the floor, I was dead! Woof!

Thomas Essex (13)
Hartshill School

Voodoo Doll

It's as weird as black magic
It's as freaky as a ghost
It's as painful as painful can be
When you look in its eyes
You hear its cries
It's a devil in disguise
With outstanding beady eyes
Its face like an Indian in disguise
It's very small not at all tall
Serious for some enjoyable for others.

Claire Benford (14)
Hartshill School

DESTRUCTION

I walked along the street,
all I saw was destruction.
I heard someone crying,
a small child was huddled.

I started to walk over to her,
but then I heard a machine-gun fire.
I scuttled onto the floor,
then slowly looked around.

That was the end of that poor child's life.
The end of misery and suffering.
I only hope I see no more,
of all this hell, upon the earth.

Shelley Morris (14)
Hartshill School

THE BOY

His hair was shiny and brown,
His eyes gleamed like twinkling stars,
He was the brightest star in my sky,
Every thunder cloud would pass him by,
But now they have taken him away,
It's not fair,
There is no shiny brown hair,
No gleaming eyes,
The brightest star has disappeared from my sky,
Now there are no thunder clouds to pass him by,
He was only small,
The boy.

Emma Sugars (13)
Hartshill School

The Followers

When I walked down the empty street,
I could hear them.
When I went into the shop,
I could sense them.
When I turned down the alley,
I could see them.
When I looked to see who was there . . .
I could feel them.
I woke in the hospital,
A broken leg, bruised ribs and black eyes.
I caused them no pain,
It's only my religion.

Siân Corbett (13)
Hartshill School

Thugs

It was a cold dark night,
The wind was blowing,
Thunder crashed like a drum.
The door swung open
And in rushed two big louts.
I was too scared to shout for help
Just in case they saw me,
I hid beneath the table
Just as quickly as they came,
They went again.

Thomas Percival (13)
Hartshill School

They Will Never Know

Our hearts are filled with sadness,
As we think of what they did.
They planted bombs in our town,
Just because of our beliefs.

My sister and my mum were killed,
And I have lost an arm.
I used to have so many friends,
But now I have so few.

The people who do this are heartless,
They just don't seem to care.
The terrorists will never know,
What it is like for us.

Elizabeth King (13)
Hartshill School

The Irish Way Of Dying

The lightning cracked,
and the thunder roared.
A bomb exploded,
and rattled through the night.
The wind was howling like
a wolf.
The rain was as loud as guns.
The hole in the road was as
big as a volcano.
I ran faster and faster,
They were chasing me,
Goodbye.

Jon Zeslawski (13)
Hartshill School

HALLOWE'EN NIGHT

H orror escaping through the doors
A fraid to go out
L ight shining everywhere
L ightning strikes again
O f one of the strangers walking by
W itches saying double double toil and trouble
E arwigs
E arwigs
N ever is sight at the old witches' houses

N ight time strikes 12 o'clock
I n the mouldy systems
G hosts!
H unting in the night
T error on the streets.

Amanda Thomas (12)
Hartshill School

LIFELESS

My daughter's life is ruined,
But no one seems to care,
That she can hardly walk or
Stand . . . or play out anymore.

She hobbles like an old woman,
But yet she's only nine,
Her young life taken from her,
And we are left with the price to pay,
Because of these cruel, cold bombs.

Stephanie Jack (13)
Hartshill School

I Was Brave And I Was Bold And Only 8 Years Old

I was brave and I was bold and I was only eight years old.
See me pass, see me dribble, see me score, what a star
Creating wonders for the Grove, making parents look so far
Now I'm older I play for England because I was brave and I was
Bold when I was eight years old.

So here is a message to all young players,
Play brave and play bold until you're 70 years old

I've played at Anfield and at White Hart Lane I've played at the Villa
In the pouring rain

I've played at Old Trafford and the City Ground,
And I would do it all again for just one pound
When
I was brave and I was bold and only eight years old.

Marc Gilbey & Matthew Hatcher (11)
Hartshill School

Hallowe'en

H allowe'en bats
A nd wicked cats
L ie down by the fire
L ights up their eyes
O n their way out
W itches come to get their cats
E very night they go out to fly
E very day all
N ight.

Shaun Philbin (13)
Hartshill School

Hallowe'en

Scary, frightening things at night,
Children screaming with the fright,
Ugly masks and bags of treats,
Witches and devils roam the streets,
Pumpkins glowing in the dark,
Even scare away the lark,
Children knock on every door,
Sometimes they become a bore,
Trick or treat is what they say,
You'd think they practised during the day,
Mars bars, Snickers, even Smarties,
All get eaten at Hallowe'en parties,
Older children love to scare,
Anyone who enters their lair,
The streets are deserted, the village is dead,
Most of the children have gone to bed,
But adults everywhere always will cheer,
Because Hallowe'en is over, well until next year.

Helen Morris (13)
Hartshill School

Hallowe'en Night

H allowe'en is very close
A ll the witches and ghosts
L ook it's raining cats and bats
L ights of illusions
O h no it's a ghost
W orms are headless
E gging people in the street
E specially ghosts
N ever say terror.

Colin Straker (13)
Hartshill School

A Winter Poem

W inter is wet, damp and cold

I cy and foggy, chilly but cold

N aughty little children go out to play
making snowmen is their idea of play for a day
T rees shaking leaves hoping to fall off today
while the naughty little children go out to play
E lephants are freezing wherever they are
people are sleeping wherever they are
R obins will sing their sweet little songs
while the birds of winter tuck up inside
because there's nowhere to hide.

Nimmy Ayilara (11)
Hartshill School

Boo!

Frogs' legs, bats' eyes, spiders and
Broomsticks all mix in for the
Ingredients for the cauldron for,
Hallowe'en. Why is there Hallowe'en?
With the cats and the bats
Especially the slimy terror of the
Wicked witches and the cats and
The ghosts, the frogs' legs and the
Bats' eyes and the children
That run around and knock on your door.
Are you afraid of Hallowe'en?

Kieran Brennan (12)
Hartshill School

Hallowe'en Nights

Flying round these winged things
With their black jagged wings
Children running round at night
Ghosts and ghouls give us a fright
Pumpkins with their scary faces
Children going to different places
Sweety wrappers on the floor
Children just want more and more
Ghosts are coming out to play
They don't come out in the day
Witches flying in the sky
You think that you are next to die
Children start to go home
Now the ghosts are all alone.

Natalie Eggison (13)
Hartshill School

Trapped

I felt terrible
In this old place
Listening to my sister scream
All in one place
My ill mother
My angry father
My sad brother
Were all in one place
I just can't stand it
Just sitting here
Starving to death.

Tara Osborne (11)
Hartshill School

Footy

They walk down the tunnel
and onto the pitch.
They get in their positions
and wait for the coin flick.
They wait for the whistle
and then they kick.

They run down the wing with the ball
with Fowler in the middle standing tall
and the crowd sing glorious for all.
Maca skips past three
and gets the cross in.
Fowler gets the ball and taps it in.

Goal!
Liverpool 2 vs West Brom 0.

Robert Morris (13)
Hartshill School

The Dark Room

I'm all alone in the dull dark room
all I can hear is bombs and
gunfire. I'm all alone in a
dull dark room. All alone
So cold and damp I've got a bed
like concrete I wish I was a
bird so I could fly away from
this war but I can't because
I'm trapped in a dull dark room.

Thomas Jones (11)
Hartshill School

The Midnight Hour

The midnight hour is close at hand,
The grandfather clock in its shadowy grave stands,
Chime, chime, crash like lightning bolts and echoing clang,
The cat's wailing with the cream cheese moon.

The devil's fork twisting and churning, red like the sun of doom,
Zombies creep and shuffle along graveyards and open the doors
of death loom.
A chilly breeze bites at your neck and objects float about the room.

The witches sweep across the skies
The black cat with green eyes
The monsters and witches are bad but they're all really sweety pies,
The dark nights with a circle of yellow are dyed by wizards' flies.
Screaming, towers of fear and chains rattling nearer, nearer and a
mortal lies.

Charlotte Dyde (13)
Hartshill School

Dear Kitty

I'm cold and tired with all this gas.
I feel sad and sick without my family.
The army drag me out to Hitler and he
shouts and shouts.
I'm angry and hungry in the cool night air.
I'm scared and upset with my life
I think it's all a dream.
But it's not a dream I'm really frightened
for once.

Lesley Mara (11)
Hartshill School

RUGBY

Rugby great,
Score a try with your mates,
Under the post kick for a goal,
Great,
Three points ahead,
Just keep your head,
Whistle blows cheers all around,
We lift the Cup,
The other team frown,
We enter the changing room,
The party begins,
They get drunk on cola,
After all those wins.

David McLoughlin (14)
Hartshill School

MY HIDEOUT

Down in the forest where I often walk,
There's a place that no one else knows,
It's my own secret hideout where
I talk to the birds, plants and my
Own special flower.
It has grown out of nothing
Among the damp green leaves,
It's beautiful it's bright
Just like a shining light.
It gives me joy to see such a sight.
One single flower standing proud, alone
How long will it last I do not know.

Ashan Chaudry (13)
Hartshill School

SILENCE

What can I hear, what can you hear, what can they hear,
I can hear the birds singing from the trees and the rooftops above,
You can hear the singing of the birds too,
They can hear nothing for they are silent,
I can hear nothing for they are silent you can't either,
I can hear the trains driving by and the
Aeroplanes as they fly.
You can hear just the same as me
They can hear nothing just silence,
I can hear silence I can hear the clock,
You can hear the clock ticking too,
They can hear the silence, they can hear
Nothing but bombs exploding around them for
They are alone their country is fighting
For them many will die.
All they can hear is the silence of the
Dead, for the dead bring silence,
Silence.

Jody Hughes (13)
Hartshill School

THERE WAS A GIRL!

There was a girl who thought she was the best,
Who said she would never need a rest,
But there was a man who could give her a test,
Mr Allban was his name he could do his best,
To get the girl from under his chest,
He asked her where she lived but guess what?
The reply was the north, south, east, west.

Danielle Clark (11)
Hartshill School

CHRISTMAS

The festive season has just begun,
With all of the gladness and all of the fun.

Snowflakes falling to the ground,
The cold wind blows the trees around.

Families gathering round the fire,
Singing softly as a choir.

Christmas trees all decorated to a 'T',
That's where the happiness will be.

Gifts exchanged and received,
Smiles on faces have been achieved.

The stockings filled to the brim,
The lights have turned to a dim.

Milk in glasses and a Christmas tart,
Puts the warmness in people's hearts.

Louisa Haddon (13)
Hartshill School

SOPHIE

She arrived one dull April day,
Like a ray of sunshine come out to play.
Her hair is blonde,
Her eyes are blue,
They sparkle just like diamonds do.
She laughs, she cries, she smiles at you,
Her brand new noise is boo, boo, boo.
Love her lots, and I am proud of
Sophie, my baby sister.

Kirk Devlin (12)
Hartshill School

Town Full Of Rain

After the storm
all night before
the world looked like
an upturned mop

Rugs outside into the wet smelly street
half dry and half wet
half dirty and half clean
tasting like old oak trees

And smelling of dogs
with their shaky fur
and cold wet noses

Scraggy cats
with spiky backs
miaowing so loud and clear
breaks all windows
Smash! Smash! Smash!

Jamie Rana (11)
Hartshill School

Disabilities

I sit in the playground all alone with no one to come and play,
I have no fun, I can't laugh or run and pray for the end of each day.
I can't climb stairs or dress myself, at home I only watch
TV and think about my health.
I have no friends because they moved away,
And no one wants to play with me because of my disability.
I know my life is soon to end, but I don't want to die without
A friend.

Ammie Stringer (11)
Hartshill School

FOOTBALL

The ball goes into the net,
The whistle blows,
The crowd cheers,
The game restarts,
The score being two-nil,
With two minutes to go,
Villa are losing,
They could go down,
But that's okay,
Because they will play another day.

Villa 0 - 2 Birmingham.

Chris Skilling (13)
Hartshill School

INDUCTION DAY

There was a school
That was so cool
I couldn't believe my eyes when I
Drew the blinds
I was shocked
With all the blocks
The hall as big as a mall
With all these rooms
I think I'm doomed
How am I going to survive
With all this on my mind?

Kerrie Dickens (11)
Hartshill School

HALLOWE'EN

Children running in the streets at night
Hoping to give people a fright
There's a knock at the door, knock knock!
You open the door and to your surprise
Five little children with a twinkle in their eyes.

Trick or treat!

Ian Parker (13)
Hartshill School

SPELL

S pooky witches fly around on their brooms
P umpkins glow as bright as the sky
E vil ghosts come out at midnight
L ightning flashes when the spirits come out
L ittle children go trick or treating to get sweets
and treats.

Chris Sadler (12)
Hartshill School

HALLOWE'EN NIGHT

Hallowe'en night is a night when you are there
for a fright. The night is here to have a cheer.
When you are in bed holding the pillow
tighter than tight. The devils scream, the
skeletons shake we are here. *ah ake*!

Barry Roberts
Hartshill School

Guns Of War

The shells of guns crash down on a city.
I listen, I hear screams of injured people.
Particles of buildings fly through the air.
A fragment of a building hits me in the
stomach and winds me.
I go to the ground and lie there 'til the smoke
of the bombs disappears.
All I can see is dead bodies and crumpled ruins.
I get up and walk away from the hunger and
poverty of war.

Chris Phipps (11)
Hartshill School

What I See And What I Feel

What I see and what I feel are
not the same in any way.

What I see is smeary and dreary
surfaces.

What I feel is sometimes good
about myself but sometimes
bad about myself.

Amy Owen (12)
Hartshill School

FOOTBALL MANIA

Giggs is running down the wing
With his arm in a sling
He does a right foot cross
But it falls to Frost

Oops, oops, oops

75 minutes gone
Beckham's scored one
Yes, yes, yes

In the end they won
One goal to none.

Gordon & Marcus (11)
Hartshill School

CHRISTMAS TIME

Christmas is a lovely time
We're playing a game it's your time to mime
The presents glitter under the tree
All wrapped up for you and me
Chestnuts popping on the fire
In the distance you hear the choir
Midnight closes in, it's nearly time
For Christmas fun to begin.

Rebecca Ewing (11)
Hartshill School

The Doctor

The doctor does his dreary test
As he looks under the old man's chest

The doctor knows what to do
When he's looking after you

That's a cold my son I'm sorry to say
You'll have to stay in bed today

Do you want a paracetamol with that
It's cold outside so wear a hat

You were feeling bad and now you're not
You can thank your doctor a lot.

Carl Fox (13)
Hartshill School

Bonfire Night

Up it goes in the air
Everyone looks up to stare
Amazing colours light up the sky
Everything amazing has to die
As Catherine wheels spin around
The night gets cold everyone goes home
Now the fire's left here alone.

Ellen Curry (13)
Hartshill School

Mr Jones

Mr Jones is kind of evil
he makes us clean up the classrooms
then he gives us a 100 lines,
just for shouting out.
And if you call him baldy
he will give you 1000 lines.
But if you're square and very nice
he will give you crisp points.

James Dunn (13)
Hartshill School

Ghouls And Ghosts

Ghouls, ghosts and spooky things,
They all seem frightening.
They appear from out of thin air,
Not really giving much care.
Under dark, damp mansion stairs,
Are where you mostly find these scares.

Nick Spittle (13)
Hartshill School

Hallowe'en Witches

Children running round at night
Tonight's the night you'll get a fright.
Ghosts and witches all around
Scaring everyone in town
Playing tricks on whoever they meet.

Lisa Bromley (13)
Hartshill School

Hallowe'en Night

Hallowe'en night is the night,
to give all the children such a fright
they go around, collecting sweets
but we all know there's death on the streets
and when they are all in a group
the shape is like a big hoop
and when they've done, dressed and ready
someone even dressed as an evil-eyed teddy.
Witches are the next thing up
they don't even drink from a cup.

Kylie White (13)
Hartshill School

Fireworks

F ireworks
I llegal sales are made to children.
R ed hot spuds are cooking nicely
E very firework goes *bang*
W illiam's throwing fireworks
  oh what a naughty boy.
O nly 18-year-olds should be buying fireworks.
R ed flashes through the sky
K eith holds his sparklers
S tars are dodging the fireworks.

Gareth Robinson (14)
Hartshill School

BRIGHT EYES

B right eyes glaring like bright lights
R eady to pounce on anybody who walks by
I n the dark you will have a fright
G lowing through the dark cold night
H ow do they pounce so high
T orturing people when they land.

E very night they hide under bushes and things
Y ellow or copper they shine in the night
E very time they see you and me
S omewhere the bright eyes are from cats.

Pascal Grant (13)
Hartshill School

BREAK TIME

The break bell rings, and the school is empty,
But outside the laughter is plenty,
Children sing and skip and run,
Everybody's having fun.
Boys play football on the ground,
Girls whisper, hardly make a sound.
But then the bell rings loud.
And they go back to school in a crowd,
In they go into school,
Nothing to do but rule after rule!

Katie Morrison (13)
Hartshill School

Alone In The Dark

All alone in the dark,
I listen to the silence,
Nothing to hear, not even a lark.

I like the way the shadows creep,
Silently floating,
They leap and leap.
As I listen to the silence,
I hear ghost music that pricks
My ears like a remembered secret -
A secret from the depths
Of the dark.

Beverley Johnson (13)
Hartshill School

Bonfire Night

Colours flying in the air
Laughing children everywhere
The bonfire roars
Fireworks sparkling more and more
Shooting stars flying
While dogs are crying
Guy Fawkes burning
While the fire is yearning
The bonfire glows
While the ice wind blows.

Sarah Keeling (13)
Hartshill School

THE NIGHT OF HALLOWE'EN

Tonight all the ghosts come out to play,
to scare the people all away.
Their evil eyes
and atrocious cries.
Look at the witch as she flies.
Screams from the graveyard
loud and eerie.
Look there goes the ghost of
bloodthirsty Mary.
Lots of candy being given away
and all the ghosts have
come out to play.

David Garrett (13)
Hartshill School

FRIENDLESS

Sitting here all alone,
Waiting for someone to come to talk.
I sit on my own every dinner,
People walk past, look and laugh.
I wish I had a friend.
In PE I'm the last to be picked.
I usually end up being partners with the teacher.
Everyone laughs.
I wish I had a friend.
I wonder what it's like to have a friend?

Rachel Coles (13)
Hartshill School

Hallowe'en

H allowe'en is very mean so make sure you're not seen.
A ngry little devils try to see how many people die.
L ittle children go around knocking on doors and speaking out loud.
L onely people in their house waiting around for something else.
O ld ghosts flying round I wonder if they touch the ground.
W itches are all around trying to make a lot of sound.
E dible things for us to eat when we play *trick or treat.*
E vil things are still out there waiting to give us quite a scare.
N obody out at the end of the night but ghosts still waiting
for one last fright.

Laura Jayne Marshall (13)
Hartshill School

Hallowe'en

H orrible hags flying through the night.
A ll the vampires looking for a bite.
L ots of ghouls and ghosts around.
L oads of spiders running on the ground.
O nly a fool would go out this night.
W itches and warlocks out for a fright.
E erie sounds and ghostly screams.
E very ghoul is out it seems
N ow your nightmare begins.

Gary Hughes (12)
Hartshill School

THE TOILET OF VENUS

The cot is soft and safe
The rich fabric enclosure warm,
Like an overgrown womb.
My back is turned to him, and I can feel
His eyes
Studying my form, my coil.
My soul laid bare, naked.
Exposed in his scrutiny.
The skin that vestures my bones,
Scrubbed, weeping and raw.

I can see myself,
My numb expression.
Such a piteous face devoid of any
Strength that it once held.
The proud features complacent,
Complying
Subject to his will.

Elizabeth Sidwell (16)
Higham Lane School

HEAVEN AND EARTH

Heaven and Earth are very different
The cold and the warm
Calm and peaceful and happy
But in Earth it is chaos, cold
Bright, poor and the rich.
Heaven and Earth are joined in unity.
In Heaven it is scented with flowers
And colourful people being reincarnated
But on Earth it is plain and simple
And the receiving of the reincarnations.

Marie Nickels (12)
Higham Lane School

The Slavery Of The Soul

The collar restricts the untamed soul,
To a dark night-time world,
Far away from the perfect blue,
The broken spirits stare desolately,
Into the disruptive swirling mass,
Around my foreign frame,
Figures dance, gambolling around the leaden cart,
Gold calls on the greedy hands,
Other captured karma writhe and squeal,
Away from the overpowering hands of man,
The hearts ricochet around the assembly,
Bumping into each other,
Causing mad moments of passion down below,
Silk brushes my nose and piggy eyes stare at my unblooded coat.
The raucous laughter contaminates the silence of the land,
Reminding us to what we are chained.

Hannah Williams (14)
Higham Lane School

The Basin Of San Marco On Ascension Day

I see narrow gondolas sliding on the water as if skating on
thin blue tinted ice.
I see crowds of unknown people determined to see the spectacle.
I see a small bridge over a river that runs through the winding
streets of Venice.
I see laughter and happiness in the eyes of the people.
I see light, puffy clouds enhancing the sky making the scene
bright and picturesque.
I see large dome-shaped buildings fading into the distance.
I see a large red boat decorated with dazzling gold with a red,
flimsy flag flying high.

Anjaljeet Sandhu (12)
Higham Lane School

THE BATTLE OF SAN ROMANO

Why when I symbolise peace
Am I surrounded by the deathly depression of war?
Constant screams surround me.
The ground stained not with the sun but with blood.
Flowing steadily further, faster, faster, faster,
Constant roar like a thousand waterfalls,
Cascading over your heart and mind.
You never see a battle but you're guaranteed to hear it.
The unmistakable sound of war,
Pounding inside your head.
People falling, fighting, dying.
Horses fall among men.
Spurs kicked into the horses' sides,
Their screams mixed with those of death.
The foul smell of war hangs in the air,
Engulfing me.
My once lily white petals, stained with blood.
A merciless sword strikes me from my stem,
My castle.
My frail body hits the ground, trampled by horses and men.
Engulfed by a pool of blood,
I see and hear no more.

Nikki Ind (14)
Higham Lane School

The Arnolfini Marriage

Take my hand and let me in
Make my mind and body spin
Shut the shutters, make them blind
Leave society behind
Throw down your hat upon your shoes
and let my lips and your lips fuse
Let my dress hang loose and free
The bulge will come back naturally
Let us do what love allows
and finish off our marriage vows.

Your face is still, a hand you raise
Be at peace it sternly says
Look not at me with unclean flame
but bow your head and feel your shame
Let the fruits of passion spoil
and so the Evil One we foil
May light stream in on your face
Society you must embrace
Make a sense of honour stay
You are my wife you must obey.

I stand before you, docile, meek
though love, affection I still seek
I am the model wife alas
my wants are locked and barred in glass.

Laura Lee (15)
Higham Lane School

The Buoy In The Thames

(From 'The Fighting Temeraire'
on the way to her last berth by Turner)

She crept past me at a snail's pace,
The steam tug straining at the leash,
I feel a pang of guilt and sadness,
As the Temeraire goes to the breakers.

The ducks quack mournfully as she drags her heels,
Melancholy, depressed, the sight makes you feel.
The tug's paddles splash on the water clear,
You can almost sense the ship's fear.

The sun dips low in the sky,
As a remnant of The Battle of Trafalgar floats by,
I gaze on, as I float,
At the sad remains of a proud boat.

An unhappy rendition of 'Rule Britannia',
Floats from the crow's nest,
The decks rock to 'Drunken Sailor',
As the morose crew have their final rum aboard the ship.

By now she's a dot in the distance,
She's going to be broken up, she hasn't a chance,
A fine ship will be destroyed
Along with sail's tradition.

David Helps (14)
Higham Lane School

The Poor Horse

As big as I seem to be
I'm really very weak.
My leg aches so terribly
I smell a horrid reek.
This disgusting man upon my back
pulls the reins so tightly.
His confidence has such a lack
to seem tall he uses me.
A storm I can smell a-coming
hangs in the misty air,
to strength I badly cling,
My life is a scary dare,
for if I move so slightly,
so slightly as can be,
he'll pull the reins so painfully
almost killing me.

Fiona Morris (12)
Higham Lane School

I Am Scared!

I am scared, I don't know what to do.
I am sitting here in school, thinking of you.
Are you hurt, or distressed?
I don't know, but I have a tickling feeling up my vest.
In that big cage all alone.
Do you need more food, or water?
I'll soon be home.
So be good, don't be bad.
You'll soon get used to me so don't be sad.
I'll soon be home, and I'll see you then,
my fluffy new hamster, little Ben.

Nadia Mubarak (11)
Hillcrest School

Bonfire Nights

B onfire nights, skies are bright,
O range flames around the bonfire,
N ever, ever put your fingers in!
F lames dancing round the sparklers
I ris-coloured Catherine wheels.
R eady for the hot dogs?
E verybody was enjoying the fireworks display.
N aughty children, shouting!
I' m glad that there was no accident.
G ot a penny for the guy?
H azelnut fire-crackers.
T ell me it is not over.
S leep tight till the next bonfire night.

Laura Hanley-Gorton (11)
Kenilworth School

What Did I See?

Was that an alien I saw creeping in the fog?
No, it was Spike, next-door's dog.

Was that a spaceship with flashing lights
in the middle of the night?
No, it was my brother riding his bike.

Was that a Martian wearing a mac?
No, it was mum in her nightie and face pack.

Was that a monster with a gruesome head?
No it was an alien at the bottom of my bed!

Hannah Merry (12)
Kenilworth School

When Will I Get There?

I was prowling
I was growling
Trying to get home
To be brushed with a comb.

Silly dogs down below
Won't catch me, oh hello
Nearly there but do I dare
To go back to my teddy bear.

I'll be kissed I'll have a hug
I'll be sat by little Doug
I will climb onto my rug
And I will be very snug.

Have you guessed yet what I am,
Cow's have calves, sheep have lambs,
But best of all it rhymes with mitten,
My mother's a cat of course, I'm a kitten.

Lisa Clifton (12)
Kenilworth School

The Flooding River - Seen From A Train Window

Big, rushing, brown and gushing.
Foaming white waves, bogged fields, submerged trees
and floating reeds.
Sinking objects, traffic cones, cans, rubbish and sign for
Wimpey Homes.
All floating and sinking, twirling and whirling,
In the mass of rushing waves.

Sophie Hunter (12)
Kenilworth School

Me, An Alien

I'm an alien I come from Mars,
I like to fly between the stars.
I have no eyebrows, skin or feet,
And fried bats' wings are what I like to eat.

My fingers are green and my nose is red,
I have lots of jelly inside my head.
I cannot laugh and I cannot cry,
I do not live and I do not die.

I do not cook for I do not eat,
I only have hands I do not have feet.
What is it like to breathe fresh air?
What is it like to always be there?
What is it like to dance play and sing?
I'm only an alien I don't know that kind of thing.

Joanne Naylor (11)
Kenilworth School

I Wonder

I wonder what it's like
to do what you like
and seeing your life flash by.
Walking through walls
to see whom I once loved
now they said goodbye.

They say it's light
and full of clouds
and down there it's red, of fear.

Laura Bailey (12)
Kenilworth School

My Alien Pal

I know an alien
from out of space
with a smirking grin
upon his face.

With great mean eyes
and a bright red nose
with purple skin and
bright green toes.

He eats whatever
he may find.
Aha! But did I
tell you he'd lost his mind?

It happened over seven years ago
and all he wanted to do was move.
Now moving's not a normal thing.

It happened because of his special ring
that has magical powers
in very tall towers
and when he went up one day
the magic ring fell away
down and down it fell
and that's how I met my pal!

Laura Evans (11)
Kenilworth School

THE ALIEN

Her big brown ugly face,
Was something of a great disgrace.

Her hair was blue and ragged and long,
And held somewhat of an unholy pong.

Her hands were smelly and dirty too,
Not something you'd want near you.

Her big blue unsettled eyes,
Were bluer than the bluest skies.

And what you wonder could this thing be,
My sister knows so don't ask me.

She only knows because it's her,
And I still wish she was how she were.

Hannah Walter (11)
Kenilworth School

TIME IS SILENT

Time is silent as can be,
I am at the beach watching the waves.
All I can hear is the waves smashing against the rocks
And the footsteps of people walking on the beach.
I like the beach. The beach has creatures.
I always sit on the beach all alone just to think things over.
I like to sit back and watch the people on the beach playing.
I sometimes make sand castles out of the sand
But what I like doing the best is listening to the echo from the shells.

Lyndsey Gallagher (11)
Kenilworth School

Bullying

Do I have to go to school Mum?
Do I really have to go,
I've got a tummy ache,
I think I'm going to throw.

They push and threaten me,
It hurts, outside and in,
They're so much stronger,
I guess I'll never win.

I couldn't sleep last night,
I was worried about what they'd say,
I have to try and ignore them,
I'll tell someone . . . one day.

Kate Holmes (12)
Kenilworth School

Silent Lottery Winner

She walked along the moonlit beach,
Careless of her belongings,
She looked and stared,
At those who cared,
Feeling the need to be free,
She had but a thousand jewels,
All spilling on the floor,
She didn't stoop to pick them up,
If she did she only lost more.
People all looked and stared,
At beauty held back from a crowd,
In her eyes the sun did not shine,
Only glistened in the moonlight.

Vicky Hill (12)
Kenilworth School

JUST A STAR?

When I gazed up at a star-filled sky,
There was one glowing pinprick which caught my eye,
Because the sight of a star has always conjured up in my mind,
Images of strange fantasies; a parallel world of some kind,
In a distant universe, light years ahead:
With quotes of Sci-Fi films brimming in my head,
'A long time ago, in a galaxy far, far away . . .'
My memories of Star Wars forever will stay,
As I stand in the garden on a cold autumn night,
The stars shine out clearly; an eternal light,
It is then that I wonder what these really are?
A planet like Venus: no ordinary star,
Perhaps part of a constellation,
Each star big enough to house several nations,
Andromeda, the Plough or maybe the Great Bear;
Whatever it is, I know that it's there.
The stars reawaken the mysticism of old,
Where fables and legends around a campfire were once told,
The destiny of myths, from Scandinavia and Greece,
Chiron the prophet or the Athenian's great fleet.
I may be accused of sentimentality,
But you cannot deny me originality,
Yes, I know you may be only a rock of fire,
As lethal as lying on a blazing pyre,
But I am still allowed to philosophise,
For nothing could lead to your demise,
And no matter what others may think you are,
To me you never could be just a star.

Leona Archer (13)
Kenilworth School

THE WINDOW

I look out of the window and see,
A beautiful world made for me,
I look out of the window, what is there?
Children playing games, happy and fair.

I look out of the window and glance,
The whole wide world has started to dance.
I look out of the window, the one by the stair
As I watch I lower my head in despair.

I look out of the window and see a world of blame
A world of sadness, a world of shame.
As I look out of the window once more
This side of the world is a place of war.

I look out of the window and tears start to fall
Others are important after all
I look out of the window, the one next to me
A smile appears at what I see.

I look out of the window the two worlds are
together
Holding hands in a circle in a hoop of peace
forever.

Chloe M Dore (13)
Kenilworth School

The Ocean Dream

The ocean swam beneath the bright orange sun,
as people walked on the beach eating their bun.
The ocean was not like a stream, it was just like
being in a dream.
The tide washed out, and the sea was calm,
as people held each other by their palms.

Amit Bagga (11)
Kenilworth School

D B Meters

I was young, a child, an innocent kid
It's a crime to tease - authority blows its lid
I go off the rails and start to be bad
Get told off, I was only being a lad.
Now I am back, with mindpower twofold
I'm not going away, like that lie you once told
Love, be loved, have fun too
Fight this hell, it's up to you!

Let's twist and shout like we did last year.
Plastic bullets - life is out, fun or fear?
Now I see, the clouds have gone.
All is lost they've already won
To defeat them is to become their kind.
Help me now, it's blowing my mind!
Death is ecstasy - a relief too.
Fight this hell, it's up to you!

I've given you my advice, there's no more to be done
Hunting the defenceless - extermination is so-called fun
Just remember me for this - the pen against the gun
We all die sometime - Judgement Day is still to come!

Benedict Peters (15)
St Benedict's RC High School

Los Desechables

I wake finding myself staring at an unjust world,
I'm not wanted by anyone here, I live in fear,
'Los Desechables' is my label, people refuse to look inside.
Nobody knows the real me, I'm trapped within a body.

Freedom! That's what I have, but this is nothing without love,
There must be someone looking down from above,
She looks down upon me, hope shines upon me every day,
This is the world to show me the way!

I breathe in the poison that supposedly relieves my pain,
Others around me believe it to be a game,
I sleep cautiously through the night until I wake in fright,
The sound of the guns is familiar to me, the sound of your misery.

Friends bring me news of hope, somebody wants to help me!
I feel apprehensive to trust, although I know I must.
This is the way to go, the correct path to follow.
I am naive, filled with optimism.

This is the only existence I've ever known, but I know there is
a better place.
I've heard of new life, another race.
I must have a destiny, a destiny hiding deep inside me,
Loss is a part of life, the turning of the knife.

Claire Dawes (16)
St Benedict's RC High School

INNOCENCE OF A CHILD

An eleven-year-old street kid
a disposable so they say
there's loads of us.
We're part of the scenery,
a fixture, a fitting

With my wall of shanty towns,
saving me or just holding me in.
I beg for some money from the people that pass,
in return for the innocence of a child's smile.

My body is hot,
but my heart and soul are cold.
We are the Parche kids.
We are our family.

The glue keeps the smile.
It hides the pain and hurt inside.
I am strong with my fake chemical friend,
No one can touch me,
Until my fake chemical friend comes to an end.

Each day I am waiting,
not for love, there's none of that in my eyes.
I am waiting but what for I don't know.

'Run' yells my friend
'The Banda are coming,
They'll shoot you dead and clear you away,
because you and I are the disposables.'

Claire Hodgets (16)
St Benedict's RC High School

Street Life

Silence has broken, gunshots.
Soldiers shouting,
as children run.
Nowhere to run,
Families have gone.

Streets are full of children
trying to get food and money.
The feeling of unhappiness and no love is looming,
as children fight for food.

Children living on scraps.
Nowhere to live.
Street gangs form sense of trust.

Living in fear.
Every day a worry.
Struggle to stay alive with loss of hope.
Soldiers prowl the area.
Machine guns fired.

Help is all they need.
Someone to trust.
Someone willing to love.

Janine Czaplinska (15)
St Benedict's RC High School

Let The Children Live

A young girl, so full of hope,
Yet she is so alone.
She has no money, no friends
Yet still she must support her sister.
The only source of love and warmth she has.

She had lived a simple, quiet life,
With her family in the country.
So beautiful she remembers,
With the glow of the midday sun,
Shining through her long auburn hair.

The day they came she will never forget,
The day that was to change her life forever.
Her mother and father both taken from them,
All for the sake of a few old animals.
She would have preferred it if the men
Had killed her too,
At least then her suffering would have been
short-lived.

With nowhere to go, she and her sister
Ran helplessly into the city.
They were alone for the first time in
their short, innocent lives.
They slept rough and survived on *rich people's* rubbish.
Treated like dirt, they had no chance in life.

Katie Thurlow (15)
St Benedict's RC High School

Los Desechables

Morning breaks and I awake.
I lie here alone with my dog.
My friend's gone in search of food,
Hounded down by the militia.
Night saw the death of José.
Only good fortune finds us here and alive.

Born ten years ago,
The youngest of four to
A violent drunken father,
And a mother who could not cope.
Three years on the streets now but alone,
My family slaughtered by gangs.

Sad and alone, with only memories of my family.
No longer there to protect and help me,
The light had gone, out of my life.
Sniffing glue and smoking marijuana is part of our lives,
It dulls the pain but quickens the anger,
In a world that's so dangerous and uncertain.

From the light and happiness in the people of the Andes,
I now find myself in the bleak depressed city.
I fight to survive in a neighbourhood,
Submerged in fear and danger.
Machine guns rattle through the night.
Girls so young on the streets, I pray for my lost sisters.

A new dawn breaks.
Help arrives!
Food, shelter, kindness?
Who can we trust?
What have we got to lose?
It's not home, but at last we've found hope!

Leisha Rymsza (15)
St Benedict's RC High School

We Live For Today

They teach us to read and write,
And help us learn a trade,
They care and love us,
And help heal our pain.

They help us move away from danger,
Physical or moral,
We live for today,
And make the most of what we have.

Some children smoke marijuana,
Gangs fight each other,
Some just give up,
But no one commits suicide.

We have highs and lows,
We pray and go to mass,
Some of us are reunited,
With family members still alive.

It can be extremely difficult,
Temperatures are uncomfortable,
We make them bearable,
In order to survive.

We live for today.

Katie Summers (15)
St Benedict's RC High School

A Life On My Own

I sit day in, day out in this damp box
On the streets of Colombia
With my shabby, begging tin placed in my hands,
Listening for the sound of coins falling, slowly, dropping,
One by one into my hands. Then . . .
I'm awoken by the sound of vehicles passing me by.

I rock back and forth, back and forth,
Trying to find warmth and comfort.
I have no family to give me love and security,
Instead glue is my only consolation.

I have many friends round here,
They're all the same as me,
Poor, young, helpless progeny.
Most of us had no option about living here.

The only way you survive the night,
Is to keep out of sight,
You can even hear the rats and mice crawling
Around,
That's how quiet you have to be.

My only desire is to turn back time,
To be with loved ones.
To have a real home, money and life.
I want to be wanted by family,
To be part of other people's lives.

Some day I will be able to have freedom,
Money of my own. And a home built like a castle.
Other people will say ' There goes the girl who was once
a disposable.'

Claire Wright (15)
St Benedict's RC High School

Los Desechables

My family fled the countryside because of war.
We built a shack from plastic and iron.
With no running water,
And no electricity.

The barrio was very violent
Many were killed each night
Father started to drink,
We had no money.
The banda burst into our shack
They shot my father in the head.

We ran away to the streets to beg,
We joined a gang and spent our money on glue
We sniffed it once,
And got hooked.
We were frightened for our lives
We did not return home.
We fought with other gangs,
The militaria populares beat people up
And killed them for no reason.

A priest saved us from the militaria populares,
He has helped us to find a new place to live,
We are learning to read and write,
We have our own bed and food,
We have given up sniffing glue.

We have a much better life now
Than we did before.

We are not 'los desechables' any more.

Hannah Baker (15)
St Benedict's RC High School

Keep Going

Yes, yes let me climb, but what when I fall?
Keep going until your highest peak until you reach your dream, not fear
The sky's the limit where clouds encourage together.
Yes, yes keep going, keep going strong, way up there,
nobody can stop you, you're as strong as a bear.
Climb on through, but where do I go?
Only you can decide for it is you in the great flow.
Help me now, I lose my grip,
please do not fear for I am there with open arms.
To guide you back like a tall great ship.
Oh rocky yes, but fearful no for I am there.
Yes, yes, go.

Paul Freeman (15)
St Benedict's RC High School

Those Eyes

I look into those eyes, and they pull me in.
Then I realise my love is about to begin.
The way she moves, the way she glides.
The way I look into those eyes.

The way she kisses so smooth and slow
I want everybody to know.
The way I care will never die and I know
my heart would never lie.

The way her hair flows this way and that,
the way it shines in the sun a bright glow.
I know my love will never die as I look
into those eyes.

Mark Moulder (16)
St Benedict's RC High School

Memories

No one promised this when I was a kid
When my days were filled with carousels
fairground rides and cockleshells
Kicking pebbles on a beach
When time couldn't reach me
And tears were just a memory left to be

Now days catch me without an overcoat
Five o'clock, shoes full of snow
All rained out, nowhere to go

Oh this winter sure gets me down
When there aren't any friends around

Memories are sure to find you
No matter how fast you run
The good memories will always catch up with you
To bring back the fun.

David Barrett (16)
St Benedict's RC High School

Looking Back

Looking back remembering how things used to be
All that pain for me
It's so easy to see.

Looking back on my life
No kids, no future not even a wife,
Seeing her again just brought it all back
Her hair, her smile and even the way she walked.

Her hair was perfect,
As good as can be.
I used to think
Me and her together for eternity.

Then it was all gone
Another man I was told.
No explanation, not even sorry
Just 'Bye bye baby where's the door?'

Oliver Mansbridge (15)
St Benedict's RC High School

Exam

It's easy son, repeated the heavy voice,
I remained quiet, hoping for help.
The room became dead,
As I stared at the text.

Completing question one, two and three,
'Easy' I thought
This is what it is all about.

The days of sacrifice pay off
I completed the test, and passed
Easy?

Five minutes of freedom and praise
Then years of work, for what?
The exam?
No, the important one is still to come!

Guy Barlow (15)
St Benedict's RC High School

Do Not Go Gentle Into That Good Night

He always told me never to give up
He should practise what he preaches.
He doesn't listen to me talking -
Just looks the other way.
He says he never knew peace in this life
Who says there will be any afterwards?
He is being so weak, but is convinced
He is doing himself and me a favour.
A good, yet an unnoticed man.
I can only watch him die.
Although in many ways, I think
His soul is dead already.
He always told me never to give up
He should practise what he preaches.

Kathy McGreal (12)
St Benedict's RC High School

A Tuesday Afternoon's Daydream

I sat and listened carefully to everything around
I sat and listened carefully to every little sound
I heard a dog start barking loudly
I heard a bee buzzing proudly
I heard the wind blowing in my face
I heard someone walk at a gentle pace
I heard a friend's cough which broke the calm still
And the rustle of leaves spoke autumn's will
I heard a bird sing merrily
I heard someone whisper 'Hello' to me
I heard the loud sound of an aeroplane roaring
And heard the soft rumble of a caravan touring
I heard the chugging of a tractor nearby
And cows mooing with indifference 'Where shall we lie?'

Amy Flint (12)
St Benedict's RC High School

A Reflection On The Past

So distant yet so clear, I can picture
the vague chubby face of a five-year-old boy.
His brown flowing hair made him resemble
a monkey. How he would climb and hang
as though his minute body defied the laws of gravity.

The solemn face, o that solemn face which appeared to be
so naive and ignorant about the petty quarrels of man.
Blue as the sea and as wide and inquisitive as a newly born
babe, yet his eyes seemed to be sad and full of grief.

Cherry red and chubby his cheeks protruded out and made,
his face fatter. His mouth was transfixed, and maintained a
gormless expression of sheer and utter stupidity. The eyes
were always awake, thinking, observing yet the mouth never
responded in accordance to the eyes.

I reflect now and remember what I had then but do not have now.
Life is different less simple, more three-dimensional. My eyes still
think for me but they do not look naive and inquisitive anymore.
They came into my world and changed it so I could no longer
think with my eyes, I was somewhere new.

I reflect and see those naive eyes and am glad, for now I know
the horrors which my childhood hid from me. I left leaving the
hate and evil behind, never knowing it or becoming a part
of it, I can reflect and recollect a happy childhood, in those
mysterious inquisitive eyes, but they are only memories now
that will always be with me.

Mark Thompson (16)
St Benedict's RC High School

Something I Am Used To

The voice I heard say 'hola'.
Not the normal voice I hear.
So kind and delicate was the sound.
Fear still made my body tense.
Fear.
Something I am used to.

The sound of respect in this voice.
Respect for me being a child.
A child, that's what I am.
Not a piece of dirt men can use, for a small expense.
Dirt.
Something I am used to.

Dare I awaken to unveil the voice.
The voice that could be an immoral, sick trick.
My eyes may meet the vision of a kind man.
Not the two holes of a gun end.
Guns.
Something I am used to.

Such a long period, that is so short.
The pain of fear still within me.
What is my destiny.
Is it good or is it bad.
Badness.
Something I am used to.

The repetitive sound of 'hola' I hear.
I open my eyes slowly.
No guns before me I see.
Could it be another degrading offer.
Degrading offers.
Something I am used to.

A white, blurred strip I see.
Rubbing my eyes, the strip becoming more clear.
It was around the neck of a priest.
It is like a dog's collar.
Dogs.
Something I am used to.

A hand, the kind man offers.
Normally I receive a shove.
Personal questions he asked.
Lies I told, small but important.
Lies.
Something I am used to.

Food and drink I was offered.
Food and drink I received.
A place of rest was suggested.
Can I force myself to trust for one night?
Trust.
Something I am not used to.

Cheryl Hathaway (16)
St Benedict's RC High School

MY DREAM BEACH GONE

Soft sand
Waves lapping
Hot sun
Breeze blowing
Children playing
Waves growing
Wind picking
Rubbish blowing
Dream beach has gone.

Kimberley Hiles (12)
St Joseph's School

MEMORY BEACH

Remembering,
Calm green sea
Remembering,
Jackie and me.

Searching,
For fish that fly,
Searching,
For shells nearby.

Thinking,
Of the golden sand
Thinking,
Of the sand on which the seagulls land.

Coming back,
To a polluted sea
Coming back,
There's no Jackie with me.

Looking around,
There's nothing there
Looking around,
The sky is bare.

Amandeep Johal (12)
St Joseph's School

The Beach

As I walk along this beach
I feel the wet sand beneath my feet.
Although it may be cold
I remember all the old stories I once was told.

The beach used to be a happy and lovely place to be
But now this beach is very sad
Mankind has been very bad
Powering waste into the sea
Making me feel very sad.

As I look around I see all the litter
It makes me feel very bitter
It's so unfair
We should have been more aware.

Penny Smith (12)
St Joseph's School

Murderers

The rippling waves all calm and free,
Hold a life beyond you and me,
From tiny fish to the great killer whale,
And the dolphin with the wiggling tail.

But now!

The waves are still rippling all calm and free,
But the life inside is as dead as can be,
With waste of all sorts and chemicals too,
We've ruined a habitat, creatures and all.
Just face it us humans are m*urderers!*

Narelle Callaghan (13)
St Joseph's School

The Sea

As I lie on the beach
I can hear the waves slowly rolling to the shore
I feel calm and tranquil.
Suddenly I lose the warm feel of the sun,
The sky goes grey, it starts to rain.

I return the next day,
I find the sand untouched,
Waiting for me to step on its smooth surface.
I walk down to the shore,
I see oil sitting on top of the sand.
Fish lying dead,
The sea a brown colour,
Seaweed washed up on the shore as high as my knee,
Suddenly I realise what man has done to nature,
I don't want to swim any more.

Alex Wagstaff (12)
St Joseph's School

My Beach

My beach would be in a far-off land
Where the ground was covered in golden sand.
The sea, not a sound nor a ripple in sight
Which for me, I suppose, would be just right.

The colour of the sea is the freshest blue
Where tropical fish pass, as if on cue.
The palm trees line the beach with green
Which altogether makes it my paradise dream.

Natasha Jeffs (12)
St Joseph's School

The Sea

The last deck chair had been stacked,
The last sand castle had been cracked,
The last hot dog had been sold,
Autumn was already a month old.
No one for miles, just me, no crowd.
All is silent but for the waves so loud,
They crash on the rocks, they rise in the air,
They lap the great wall they wet everywhere.
The sand is so soft, so clammy, like clay;
The air is so damp, so full of sea spray.
Above on the skyline the odd seagull does fly,
Screeching to his mate 'Quick winter is nigh.'
The fairground is still, just like a ghost town,
The rides under cover, all securely tied down.
Another year's over and summer long-gone.

Carolyn Bradley-Winnett (12)
St Joseph's School

Paradise

I walk across the smooth white sand,
The large green coconut feels cool in my hand.
When I look round, all that I see
Is the empty beach, palm trees and sea.

I sit down all alone, with the peaceful sound
Of the seagulls and the waves all around.
I cannot think of a more wonderful place
Than the one that I call 'paradise'.

Lucy Greville-Smith (12)
St Joseph's School

THE SEASIDE

The tide was growing and growing
Higher and higher it went
Everyone eating fish and chips as they went
by.

Seagulls were crying because the wind was so
strong,
Each and every one trying to get a hiding
place,
All around the sea went calm,
Sitting by my window I saw all of this,
It turned into sudden happiness,
Dogs running in and out of the sea, then all
of a sudden,
Empty - it all went empty.

Sarah Warn (12)
St Joseph's School

THE SEA

I love the sea.
The golden sand.
The waves rush back to the
shore like clashes of
thunder.
The seashells look beautiful
on the shore.
The sea animals dance in the sea.
I tease my mum with
seaweed.
The sea is very calm at night.

Maria Murray (12)
St Joseph's School

The Seaside

I walk along a cold wet beach,
On a miserable blustery day.
The sea is roaring here and there
In its own noisy way.
You can hear the sea crashing on the rocks like thunder,
And then quietening down again.

The seagulls dive
To and fro
Trying to find fish
In the big tossing waves.
The day is nearly ending
And I wish tomorrow
Will be warm and shining.

Emily Murden (12)
St Joseph's School

Sounds At The Beach

As I run towards
The soft silk sand,
As the sand runs through my toes,
I hear the gently lapping sea.

I hear a noise,
Up I look
Just to see the gulls.
I can also hear laughter,
I look down
To see the children playing.

Emily Farley (12)
St Joseph's School

The Beach

I am walking on the beach,
the sand is so soft beneath my feet.
You can hear the waves crashing on the rocks.
I can smell the salty seawater,
and the hot dogs and beefburger stands,
up the sea front.
The water is so nice and cool upon my feet,
the seaweed is slimy and green.

It is getting cold,
it looks like rain.
The sea has changed from blue to grey.
I feel a splash on my head,
and then another it is starting to rain.
I'd better go in or get soaked.
Looking out of the window,
the sea is getting rough.
Never mind it will all be calm again tomorrow.

Amy Browne (12)
St Joseph's School

A Poem About The Beach

The calendar turned for another day
I walked my dog along the bay,
Among the bed of golden locks reflecting
of the sunset rocks.
The orange shadow still set in the sky
the endless night that never goes by
The sea claps its hands together,
to form a giant wave which lasts forever.

Jackie Little (12)
St Joseph's School

My First Day At My New School

Last week as I recall
Was when I went to my new school

I walked in through the big iron gate
Oh no! The bell's gone, I'm gonna be late

I ran inside as fast as I could
But I think that was faster than I should

The teacher took me by the arm
And said, 'To the Head' I had raised alarm!

I slowly walked to my new class
The teacher said, 'Let's go out and sit on the grass.'

All day long we sat on the grass
Doing our lessons whilst time passed

At last the teacher said it was time to go
I packed my bag but I was too slow

The rain came down all over my books
Oh no! What will the teacher say when she looks?

Amanda Rees (11)
St Joseph's School

The Four Seasons On Magaluf Beach

Summer is always hot and exotic
The sand is all silky and smooth
There's no fail, you'll always have fun
Even if you're just lying in the sun.

Autumn is time to put those swimsuits away
The sea starts to get chilly
The wind gets up more speed
And *boom!* Winter comes to lead.
Winter can be cold and wet
The sand is all damp and sticky
But you could always sit
In the beachside restaurant.
Or you could wander off and go
Shopping in the Court D'ant.
Spring can be warm and pleasant
Everywhere is starting to liven up
The sea gets warmer
The wind also gets calmer
And the welcome of summer arrives.

Kelly Louden (12)
St Joseph's School

WATCHING

I look across the sea,
Where does it end?
Waves are dancing their usual dance,
Little white fairies are lying upon
Each little wave.

The sky is getting darker
The sea creatures are hiding,
And I am still watching
Them prance away.

The sun settles down
The moon lights up,
The sea is alive and bright
With the reflections of the sparkling stars.

Now in the morning
The sun is awake,
The sea creatures dance
And swirl through the sea.

A new day has begun
And I am excited about what is ahead.

Stephanie Laird (12)
St Joseph's School

As I Walked Along The Beach

As I walked along the beach one day,
The sea was calm and blue,
The sky had cotton wool buds floating in it,
The beach looked like a path of gold
That people hadn't yet seen.

As I walked along the beach one day,
The sea was lapping on the sand,
Slip, slap, slip, slap.
I could hear the gulls calling to each other,
Fishing in the sea.

As I walked along the beach one day,
I could smell the sea, the salt air,
Not yet spoilt by barbecues,
Car fumes or people.
The beach was untouched by the outside world.

As I walked along the beach one day,
I could feel the sea spray on my arms,
The sand under my feet,
The cool breeze on my face
And the hot sun on my back.

As I walked along the beach one day,
I could see the black sky
Illuminated by lightning.
I could hear the crash of the waves against the piers
And the beach wasn't calm any more.

Catherine Tressler (12)
St Joseph's School

The Seaside

Heading across the open beach,
The wind swishing gently across my face,
Leaving civilisation behind me
With all the damage it has done.

The pawprints of a solitary dog,
Winding its way across the sand,
Gently pressed into the golden ground
Are washed away by the coming tide, leaving a handful
of shells in its place.

A seagull gently calls its mate,
And an answering cry is heard from far away,
The warm air is filled with the scent of salt water
And the sun announces the coming of day.

A cloud passes over the sun,
An angry crab scuttles past,
A rumbling comes from the distance
And the waves push forward in their eagerness to reach land.

The sea becomes fierce,
The sky blackens ominously,
And the gentle scene
Turns into a ferocious monster.

Katherine Shaw (12)
St Joseph's School

My Dad's Boat

My Dad's boat
Goes boom and bounce
Over the waves we go.

The sea is rough
The air is thin,
Sun is glowing in the sky,
Sunglasses on.

My Mum's in shock from bounding
Over the sea
Under and over the waves we go.

The sea air is bitter and cold
Four jumpers on,
Four coats on,
Zipping of coats,
Clicking of life jackets,
Click, click, click and a zip.

Sea's getting bad
Every bang rattles your ribs
Four people screaming
Me and Mum screaming the loudest.

We are in danger
A big red lifeboat is coming
Over the big waves.

He gives us a rope,
And tows us back
To the water's edge

Four people safe
The adventure is over
Home sweet home.

Katy Bennett (11)
St Joseph's School

My Grandpa

Is that my grandpa
in that outstanding uniform
of navy blue?
Was he in the war?
I'm so sure he was.

Look at the flowers
in gran's hair.
And the happiness shared
around the family.

Those silk white dresses,
hats and veils.
The navy stripes of white
the young and old faces.

I wonder what he'd be
like if he was still
alive today.

Stephanie Brown (12)
Southam High School

My Nan

So happy sitting upon that bench
And behind her a wooden fence.

Smiling as she always does
Because mum needs a lot of love.

How old would she be
With young mum upon her
knee?

Alison Jackson (12)
Southam High School

Grandpa

He looks so peaceful, sitting there in his own little world,
Wearing the old brown coat he always wore,
Though I can't see his hands, a fishing rod he must have held,
Of fishing he never seemed to bore.

What was he watching that's just out of view?
What was he thinking as he sat in the cold?
The water of that lake looked so blue,
Why did he go when he wasn't that old?

Who was behind that camera that day?
Bobbing up and down in the small boat,
Looking intently over the hills and far away.
'Keep still and calm' he seemed to quote.

Carla Iliffe (12)
Southam High School

Memories Of My Mum

I wonder if this grass is tasty,
Quick, I'd better make it hasty.
Yum, yum that grass is nice,
And it looks like tails of mice.

I've just had my hair cut,
And had a new dress,
If I get it dirty my mum will stress.
I wonder what my mum is thinking,
I suppose no one will ever know.

Gemma Florida (12)
Southam High School

VAMPIRE

The night was dark,
the moon was limp.

The vampire awakens,
he feels severely hungry.

He arises from his underground den,
he sets off to seek his victim.

As he stalks around the silent city,
it's then he sees an open window,
up the drainpipe he goes.

He sees her lying there, sleeping soundly,
his eyes turn a mysterious red.

He clenches his teeth into her neck,
as the blood flows, the vampire's
energy regains.

When the girl is drained from her blood,
the vampire felt the urge to fly,
he turned to a bat and over the
horizon he flew.

Carly Allum (13)
Southam High School

DEMON

D ark, deadly and devious
E vil, frightening and mischievous
M agically, monstrously, taunting
O range, gleaming eyes haunting
N ever to be messed with.

Adam Wilson (13)
Southam High School

VAMPIRE

In the dead of night he rises
above the city he flies.
He seizes his sleeping victim
and in the distance you hear painful cries.
As the cloaked figure leans over
his fangs pointed like a shark's,
he sucks until he's had plenty,
and then silently departs.

Back to his resting place he crawls,
to his coffin underground,
he's been out searching for
some blood like a bloodthirsty hound.

Sarah Talbot (13)
Southam High School

POLTERGEIST

P ulling along the
O pen coffins
L asting for all
T ime, torturing
E verything
R esting against the
G ravestones
E ternity
I n the everlasting cold
S top everything and
T hink.

Sarah Glover (14)
Southam High School

HORROR

H orribly disfigured, an
O gre in every way
R ampages violently
R eaping havoc wherever he goes
O n and on he leaves his victims
R ipped limb from limb

S hadows are where he likes to hide
T errifyingly gruesome
O ut of the shadows he pounces
R oaring ferociously
Y et he remains at large.

Simon Dommett (13)
Southam High School

MEMORIES

Is that Dad, is that Grandad?
Is that the size he really was?

Are they having fun?
Does my Dad want to run?

What did they really do?
Was my Dad missing a shoe?

Was he a little joker?
But he now plays a good game of poker.

David Rowley (12)
Southam High School

THE VAMPIRE!

The mist rolls in as darkness falls.
Time for Dracula to make his nightly calls.
Dressed in black, his cape flowing in the wind.
He waits to strike, his fangs glowing,
for his victims to pass, as yet unknowing,
of the horror he feels, as his blood starts flowing.
Victims freeze in terror, unable to fight,
or try to escape, the blood-sucking bite.

The horrors of darkness came to a height,
with the calm of the morning's welcome first light.

As the sun warms the day, the hunters are brave.
As the vampire lies asleep safely in his grave.

Nicholas Holland (13)
Southam High School

THE VAMPIRE

The vampire's bright he comes out at night,
To scare all the people away.
He likes to bite and make people fright,
A horrible Lamia is he.
The vampire's yawning it's nearly morning,
For light is not for he.
He won't bite till another night,
But who knows who the victim may be!

Rob Milburn (13)
Southam High School

THIRSTY

He rose from the murky grave,
Like a decaying piece of meat,
Looking for an unfortunate slave,
Shuffling along on his tiny feet,

He moves along the tiny town,
Making no noise going down the road,
Looking for a window and a girl in a gown,
Following his own vampire code,

He spots a house with a light in its window,
Moving towards it with thirst in his eyes,
He has to get there and put his fangs on show,
And make sure that his victim dies,

She lay on her bed, her eyes firmly shut,
He leant in to take a bite,
Then on her neck appeared a deep cut,
And with that came her last glimpse of light.

Laura Rawlings (13)
Southam High School

VAMPIRE

V enomous vampires
A re ready to suck your blood.
M an or bat or maybe both.
P eople are victims, victims of greed.
I n coffins they live.
R eady to suck your blood.
E mpty vampires will suck you dry.

Adam Smith (14)
Southam High School

VAMPIRE

With skin white as snow,
And sharp teeth gleaming,
He flies into the night,
With black cloak streaming.

The innocent victim lies asleep,
And into the room the vampire creeps.
In his mighty pursuit of blood,
He does not hear the door go *thud.*

He does not see the splintered stake,
Till it darts at him like poisoned snake.
Pain runs through him like a dart,
As the stake runs deep, straight through his heart.

Hannah Lee (13)
Southam High School

UFO

The bright object in the sky,
Hovers over for some time,
Bright lights flash around and around,
Light shining on the ground,
Sucks up any living thing it sees,
What happens next is beyond you and me.
Two hours later you're back on ground,
But there is nothing to be found,
You tell people what you've been through,
But they only laugh and don't believe you.

Samantha Meredith (13)
Southam High School

VAMPIRE'S RECRUIT

Rising as silently,
As a tiger upon his prey,
A soulless executioner,
Coming out to play.

Unsuspecting victim,
Unconscious of the fact,
That an evil corpse,
Is about to attack.

In sink his teeth,
The blood begins to flow,
Then as swiftly as he came,
He silently turns to go.

Following out of the window,
In quick pursuit,
The newly drained victim,
Becomes his new recruit.

Becky Busby (13)
Southam High School

COFFIN

C old and creepy,
O ld and sleepy,
F rightening and sneaky,
F ound
I n the ground
N ext to Mr Mound.

Samantha Cowley (13)
Southam High School

VAMPIRES

A vampire's teeth are like bright bars
They come out at night just like the stars.
They sink into a person's neck
And reduce them to a quivering wreck,
They suck the blood from a person's veins,
And another vampire is all that remains.

A clove of garlic and a crucifix
Are not ingredients he will mix,
You are only safe throughout the day
Because in a coffin he will lay.
The only way to kill this human fake
Is to pierce his heart with a stake.

And in my conclusion may I say
Beware and try to keep this spectral being at bay.

Gemma Reeves (14)
Southam High School

VAMPIRE

V icious eyes glow red
A s midnight strikes he rises from a coffin and
M akes his way through the
P itch black night, he sees his
I nnocent victim and makes his violent attack
R aging as he drinks every last drop of blood leaving an
E mpty carcass behind as he returns to his dark grave.

Alison Morris (13)
Southam High School

THOMAS KEMPE

Be gone oh spirit of the night,
Before the sun brings daily light.

Tail of rat, wing of bat,
Leg of cow, ear of sow
Eyes of frog, beetles from a log
A fish's scale, a baby whale.

Be gone oh spirit of the night
Before the sun brings daily light.

A mountain goat, a pink raincoat
One red rose, a fox's nose.
A swan's orange beak, snow from a mountain peak
A lion's claw, a dog's paw.

Be gone oh spirit of the night
Before the sun brings daily light.

Liz Bench (14)
Southam High School

NIGHTMARE

N ervous exhaustion
I nvites restless nights.
G remlins creep in,
H obgoblins and nastiness
T orment half-consciousness.
M acabre happenings
A waken with a jolt.
R estless nights
E ndure forever.

John Perry (13)
Southam High School

THE VAMPIRE

The vampire awakes
he needs a drink of blood
he searches through the city
and there his victim stood.

He follows round the corner
but there, out of sight, she's gone.
He walks away
but won't leave until his work is done.

He sees an open window
and climbs right in.
There he sees his victim
the deep sleep she's in.

He lashes out at her
and there she shouts a cry
and there is a silence
she does not want to die.

Now his work is finished
he's not thirsty any more.
He doesn't care, he hurt her,
about all the skin he tore.

Zoe Carroll (13)
Southam High School

THE VAMPIRE

Waiting in his tomb till night,
Then his eyes light up bright.
Flying high on passers-by,
When he pounces they will die.

He flies in the night,
He gives you a fright.
He scares you to death,
Or is it his bite.

John-Paul Ellis (13)
Southam High School

The Vampire

His eyes so red and evil,
His fangs so sharp and white,
His black cloak is billowing,
As he glides on through the night.

He glides towards the city,
To find the perfect host,
As the bells toll midnight,
He lands silent as a ghost.

He spies a window open,
He slowly creeps inside.
Upon the bed in slumber,
A lonely maiden lies.

Her neck so white and slender,
Invites him to take his fill,
He takes all he desires,
Her body lies limp and still.

The hours have gone by,
Dawn is about to break,
He must never cast a shadow,
For his coffin he must make.

Catherine Priest (14)
Southam High School

The Vampire

The vampire rises from his grave,
To seek a suffering victim.
He glides across the dark night sky,
Searching for someone to feed him.

He spots a sweet young girl,
Who's standing by a small shop,
And swoops down to his victim,
And drinks her blood like he'll never stop!

He leaves his fully-drained victim
His work is completely done.
Then gliding back up to the sky,
He laughs, 'cause to him it's just fun!

Natalie Rabôt (13)
Southam High School

Vampires

V ampires
A lways stalk their victims, always
M aking them
P rey!
I n their necks he bites through hard,
R eleasing the blood, sucking it out, then
E ventually going back to his epitaph until he
S trikes again!

Shanne Rawbone (13)
Southam High School

THE VAMPIRE

Somewhere in the cold night air,
A vampire lurks beware, beware.
Feeling weak it knew the need,
To leave its grave, for a nice long feed.

This vicious and terrifying beast,
Is searching for a person on whom to feast.
Just one quick and well-placed bite,
Can and will end all your fright.

Upon finding somebody it'll drink its fill,
And leave its victim cold and still.
For when they awake they'll know one thing,
Their thirst for blood, not the pain it will bring.

Sam Cronin (13)
Southam High School

DRACULA

On a cold and dark night,
I heard a noise, it gave me a fright.
A shadow fell upon my bed,
I daren't breathe or move my head.
My heart was beating very fast.
I knew he'd come for me at last.
I could feel his breath on my neck.
I felt a little peck.
The blood ran out onto his fangs,
And now I'm in his little gang.

Dan Houghton (13)
Southam High School

The Vampire

The vampire, he is thirsty,
He needs a drink of blood.
He's looking for a victim,
Behind his big dark hood;
He creeps around the city,
It's silent and it's dark.
He's startled by a noise,
He hears a big dog bark;
He finds an open window,
He climbs in it with ease,
He finds himself in a bedroom
And a victim asleep he sees.
He walks up to the body,
And pushes back her hair,
He goes towards her neck,
And there she lies and stares.
He runs, he's out the window,
He finds another house,
He creeps up to the window
As quiet as a mouse.
He climbs into the window
And quietly he goes.
He leans over the body,
She's smelling like a rose.
He bites deep in her neck,
And sucks out all the blood.
He runs out of the window,
Behind his big dark hood.

Sharon Joyce (14)
Southam High School

VAMPIRES FEED

Vampires come out at night
Planning to give someone a fright.

Blood pouring out of the victim's neck
In the next minute he is dead.

The darkness is going
The sun is coming

The vampires are running
Back to the darkness.

Where he will wait
Until his next awakeness.

Luke Facer (13)
Southam High School

THE VAMPIRE

A shadow moves across the street
The person behind the shadow is swift on his feet
It must be looking for something to eat
It climbs up a drainpipe and goes in an open window
It finds a sleeping widow
A shout and a scream then nothing
Then a loud voice shouted 'Vampire!'

Chris Corkhill (13)
Southam High School

Vampire

The vampire hovers and stalks every night
He's really thirsty, then people catch his sight
He goes down to them to chat them into staying
He lets them in to have tea with him.

Then one by one he takes a bite in their neck
He sucked out their blood, the room looked a wreck
The dead bodies suddenly come alive
Walking like zombies staring outside.

Slowly towards their coffins they lay down
They are vampires now, it was all silent around
Soon the vampires will enter again
They will linger and stalk through the night
Until some people catch their sight.

Coral Tassi (13)
Southam High School

The Vampire

The night is dark and still,
and out from the dark and gloom
arises the vampire.
His skin is white, his eyes
are deadly and evil,
his one and only desire
is blood, and from
the shadows comes the
vampire. *Beware!*

Becky Bennett (13)
Southam High School

Vampire

He awakes slowly,
Wondering who's about,
He climbs from his coffin,
He feels thirsty, he needs a drink.

He walks through a graveyard,
Reading the epitaphs,
He sees a girl,
She's crying and standing by a grave.

His eyes light up.
'My prey' he thinks.
He can't control himself,
All he can think of is blood!

He makes his way over to the girl,
Silently, trying not to make a sound.
The girl turns round,
She screams and runs.

He runs after her,
On and on through the darkness.
He can hear her crying,
Shouting for help.

The girl trips,
He hovers over her.
'What do you want ?' says the girl.
'Blood' he replies, as he goes for her throat.

Abby Pink (13)
Southam High School

VAMPIRE

As the night drew late
When everyone's asleep
One man lay in wait
For anyone he meets.

He only comes out at night
To give his taste buds delight
A man is coming home late
That's when the horror takes place.

One big gush of blood will do
It will take him through
Until it comes to you.

David Waddell (13)
Southam High School

VAMPIRES

The moon was full, the clock struck twelve.
The vampire comes to play with his pals.
With a big black coat and sharp fangs
High in the tree where he hangs.
There he looks with a watchful eye
Watching all the passers-by.

Ashley Hancock (13)
Southam High School

Vampire Poem

Where did all this blood come from?
Last night he was here, today he is gone
Marks on bodies, like two holes,
He drinks their blood whilst stealing their souls.

Bodies lying lifeless on the floor,
One moves, the one by the door,
She looks at me with dark red eyes,
Opens her wings and then she flies.

Closer and closer towards me,
The door is only there, could I flee?
No! I have to face my fear,
She bites my neck, I cry a single tear.

Alie Green (13)
Southam High School

Vampire

V ampire in the house,
A nd it moves towards my room,
M oving quiet as a mouse,
P ulling my hair away from my neck
and my heart goes boom.
I n go your fangs sharp and deep
R ed blood running down my neck,
E nd of my life now I'm dead!

Samantha Godfrey (13)
Southam High School

The Vampire

The vampire wakes at midnight
His stomach starts to rumble
He gets dressed and goes into town
To feed on all the humble.

No one knows he's coming
They're all tucked up in bed
But just in case he visits
They pull the covers over their heads

The vampire gets excited
When he sees an opened window
And when he looks inside the house
He finds a frail old widow

With her knitting in her hand
The widow had fallen asleep
And apart from quiet snoring
The vampire couldn't hear a peep

He took one last look at the widow
And wondered if he should
But he dug his teeth into her neck
And sucked as hard as he could.

Alan Amaira (13)
Southam High School

Vampire

He walks through the city looking
for a snack. A nice cheeky corpse will
do for his bitter taste.

His teeth are so sharp and long
to puncture a nice fleshy neck.
He doesn't care if they squeal
for then he breaks their neck.

He flies through the window
into a rich room for there is
a cheeky girl there frightened for her life.

In one strike the girl is dead
then off he flies back to his
dusty box waiting for night-time again.

Kieren Bodill (13)
Southam High School

THE VAMPIRE

His weak and pathetic body
Hides away in the gloom.
He grins to himself grimly,
As the vampire leaves his tomb.

His eyes are red with evil,
His teeth are white as white.
As he walks towards the city,
In the middle of the night.

So through the streets of the city,
He makes his individual way.
He's stumbling along silently,
To make his victim pay.

At last he finds his victim,
Lying silently in the park.
He digs in quickly and to his delight,
It's the two of them alone in the dark.

His not so pathetic body
Hides away in the gloom.
He grins to himself grimly,
As the vampire returns to his tomb.

Lucy Beeston (13)
Southam High School

The Vampire

The vampire woke quite early,
In fact there was still light.
So he sat behind a gravestone,
Waiting for the night.

One by one his friends emerged,
Happy to be free.
They walked across the graveyard,
Then hid behind a tree.

Around the corner came some youths,
They were drinking wine.
By luck the youths were so drunk,
The vampire didn't dine.

The vampires carried on
Until they came to the church.
They crept inside to have a peep
And for the healthy they did search.

They grabbed their victims by the leg,
And pulled them all outside.
Then they slowly drank the blood,
And the new vampires sighed,

I want blood!

Tim Welby (13)
Southam High School

VAMPIRE

The vampire wakes,
He smells the blood,
He rises from his spectral grave,
And stalks the town.

This victim is perfect in every way,
The blood is perfect,
The neck bare,
He bites!

Walking through the graveyard now
There are two figures, not one,
They both seem to disappear,
In their place, two bats.

Matt Hill (13)
Southam High School

THE VAMPIRE

He moves in closer to his victim
ready to pounce.
He jumps in and rips the victim apart,
bursting for a pint of blood!
The victim shrieks as he digs in deeper.
He leaves the victim lying on the cold floor
as cold as a leaf.
He returns to his home at the back of the city
to plan his next attack.

Mark Higgs (13)
Southam High School

SHEETS OF BLOOD

Sleeping innocently,
Below the white sheets,
A pale pretty face,
He meets.

She stirs unknowingly,
In a world of peace.
Was this the rent
Upon her lease?

A bite like a dagger,
In her small neck,
Draining her blood,
Her life he will wreck.

She screamed out loud,
Unable to defend,
This one the doctor,
Will be unable to mend.

His thirst has left,
He pulls away,
Leaving her to face,
A wicked day.

Charlotte Rudge (13)
Southam High School

THOMAS KEMPE - THINK AGAIN

Bubble, bubble, get rid of your trouble,
You left my life in a heap of rubble.

Fire burn and bat's eye firm,
Read the notes and you will learn.

Thomas Kempe think again,
Go away or die in pain.

Tongue of dog, nose of frog,
Mix all these up and heart of hog.

Fire burn, fire hot
Lizard's tongue and dragon snot.

Fire burn and bat's eye firm,
Read the notes and you will learn.

Fire burn, fire hot,
In ancient times he was forgot.

Get eye of mouse and birdie's song,
Not long now and he'll be gone.

Mix all up in a pool,
Then Thomas Kempe will always be forgot.

Fire burn, bat's eye firm,
Read the notes and you will learn.

Katie Alsop (13)
Southam High School

VAMPIRE

In the deepest darkest part of the night,
That's when this terrifying creature
comes out to hunt,
In the blackest most deserted place
is where its prey awaits,
Its prey is not just any old animal,
but a special one indeed,
For bears and rabbits are
not what it hunts but humans'
blood it drinks,
Just the sight of a bare neck
can make its gruesome mouth water,
And make its physical strength
10 times stronger that a human's,
A little bite is all it takes to
drain a human's body of blood,
When it has fed there will be
10 dead humans,
But 10 newborn vampires,
For that is the creature I've been telling you
about in this little poem,
And know this also, for it is the
most important thing of all,
When that vampire feels hungry again
it will be out for *more!*

Deborah Williams (13)
Southam High School

THE SPELL OF THOMAS KEMPE

To get a ghost that
is annoying you,
Get a bottle and make a stew,
Fill it up with lots of things,
From frogs' legs and toads
and bats with wings,
Add some water and some spice
with some sugar to make it nice,
When you have done this put
in the cork,
And make sure you get your
knife and fork,
Then it's time to give it a shake
and put it in the oven for it
to bake,
Leave it in the oven for one
whole day,
Then when you get it out don't
forget to say,
'Thomas, Thomas come to me,
Here is a lovely poison come
and see,
Have a look all inside
There is no need for you to hide,
Take off the cork and have a sniff,
I'll go away and be back in a jiff.'
Ha, ha my spell has worked
Thomas has fallen in,
I will put on the cork
And throw him in the bin.

Alan Guilford (13)
Southam High School

VAMPIRES

The vampire laughed,
as he made his path,
through the muddy wood,
to the cheerful pub.

As he walked in,
he found his victim within,
She had long flowing hair,
and she gave him an ugly stare.

He walks across and grabs her hand,
and asked her to walk the beautiful land,
He gave her a cuddle,
and she made not a struggle.

Then his eyes became bright,
and he gave her a fright,
He opened his mouth,
and leant to the south.

He took a bite from her neck,
she fell over and hit the deck,
She lay covered in mud,
and dripping with blood.

She now was a vampire too,
She just did not know, what to do.

Rachel Wandod (13)
Southam High School

IF

If I could have three wishes,
The three wishes would be,
To meet my best pop star,
To have lots of money,
And the last wish would be,
To travel around the world.

If I have a fourth wish
I would take you with me.

Samantha Rowley (14)
Sparrowdale School

I WISH I COULD BE A WINNER

I wish I could be a winner,
Poems, stories or in magazines
In all competitions.
If I do win a competition,
I would be over thrilled.
So please make me a winner,
It would change my life.

Stevan Ptaszynski (14)
Sparrowdale School

Too Small

Bouncy, bouncy basketball,
I like to play but I am too small.
I have to dribble under their legs,
And knocked them over like wooden pegs!
Bouncy, bouncy basketball,
I like to play but I am too small.

Matthew Mitchell (13)
Sparrowdale School

There Was A Little Boy

There was a little boy,
Who sat on a chair eating porridge.
There came a rat who scared the boy away.

He ran to tell his mother.
His mother came with the cat.
And the cat chased the rat, and they didn't see it again.

Anna-Marie Cheshire (13)
Sparrowdale School

How?

How can I write a poem?
How can I get to win a prize?
When I'm not very good at writing
And I'm not very good at drawing.
But I try.

Steven Cousins (14)
Sparrowdale School

SPELLBOUND

Soaring up,
Reaching its peak.
Curling over,
Tumbling down.
Like a flock of white doves soaring, gliding to the shore.
Its tremendous stature was simply astounding
grasping towards the sky.
The sun's glistening rays reflected off of the crisp,
clear blue surface.
In one sweeping movement the waves came crashing down,
overwhelming in strength and power,
churning the sand along the shore.
The doves coast their final inches,
becoming sucked back.
Struggling to reach their end.
The sea like one huge mouth breathing in,
just about to sneeze.
Then one after another with such
awesome force they start again
Competing to be the best
Higher and higher
Towering over me
Eventually engulfing me.

Katie Shelton-Smith (14)
Stratford High School

Spellbound

For me, being spellbound is the sight of a shooting star
Racing through our skies
Being spellbound is the sight of Hale-Bopp
A magical ball of fire.

A cold night was its arrival in my sky
As I stood under the moonlight, a sense of immense astonishment
held me
But then its mystery unfolded before my eyes
A wonder of our infinite universe.

My amazement grew as I focused on this silent giant
An assortment of colours, like a rainbow
Its tail following its mighty leader
Dodging fellow white, shining stars.

And then the fact dawned on me
Watch it while you can!
For this wonder will not be seen again for many centuries
When, again, its magic will leave us spellbound.

Amy Bishton (14)
Stratford High School

Spellbound

I stood transfixed and watched the light
I felt bemused; it was too bright
The smell of cordite; the sudden noise
Held amazed the girls and boys.

I looked and saw reflections on faces
From different times and different places
All bewitched and dazzled by what they saw
To those not knowing, it could be a war.

Suddenly from the front of the crowd
A flash of white, a sound so loud
Something rushed upwards and exploded on high
I remembered to breathe and exhaled a sigh.

It was a magic moment filled with light
And I will always remember my bonfire night.

Kate Harrison (14)
Stratford High School

MAGIC PIGGY

I have a little secret, I keep it to myself,
I have a magic piggy he sits upon my shelf.
When all the house are sleeping he jumps upon my bed,
His tail a little curly his eyes a pinky red.
He twitches his ears, he taps his toes,
The spell is set and off he goes.

Up into the spellbound sky,
My little piggy he does fly.
He gives his greetings to the stars,
A big hello to the man on Mars.
He has a chat with Mr Moon,
Promising to be back soon.

Opening my eyes, piggy's on the shelf,
I had a pleasant dream, I keep it to myself.
Looking out the window I see a lovely sight,
Where once the moon was gleaming, the sun is shining bright.
My mother says that pigs don't fly,
But who am I to question why?

Lisa Fernandes (12)
Stratford High School

Snow Bear

Snow white
Snow bright
White polar bear
Shadows do fall on the ice
But there is nothing there.

Followed throughout to burning snow
Flickering with the flame
The beauty that I saw there did not have a name.

One, two, three
Pairs of eyes did see
See me turn and walk away
For there I could not stay.

Only the shadow lives on
Singing its one, sad, sad song
The reason why
I could not stay
A friend and a bear
Were killed that day.

Charlotte Pearce (13)
Stratford High School

The New Arrival

Gorgeous deep blue eyes struck me with their vacant stare,
Emotion filled up inside me,
I was dazed by an unusual air,
The pinch I gave myself brought me shuddering to reality.

I wanted to relish this moment forever,
The beautiful new arrival was filled with as much curiosity as I was,
Her intense smile ran through me.
I carefully picked up the bundle of pleasure,
I acted on impulse and eagerness.

Marvelling at her tiny pale nose.
A deep impression sunk into my heart,
I watched as she adopted a more comfortable pose.
She looked up and smiled, it was hard for us to part.

Emma Jones (14)
Stratford High School

Cardboard Box

The air is cold on this London street,
Newspaper in my jacket.
Some bits down at my feet,
In my hat there are a few pennies.
On it a badge of two doves,
In my pocket a crust of bread.
On my hands my worn-out gloves.
I left home at 14 now I'm 15,
One year on the street.
It's hard, I've no job.
I ask for money from the people I meet,
And I'm sitting in a cardboard box.

I've just woken up to the sound of a fight,
There's usually one going on.
They can keep you awake all night,
It's time to go look for work,
I might go visit my friends.
But they might not want me around
I'll just stay,
Sitting in a cardboard box.

Katherine Latham (13)
Stratford High School

SUNSET AT THE GRAND CANYON

Stood at the fringe of the Canyon,
My anticipation was roaring to be set free.
Watching, waiting;
What was I waiting for?
Self-contentment was my desire.
Would I find it here?
Here in the earth's natural monument of magic?
As the ball of fire begins to fall,
my anger starts to melt.
I felt peace and contentment.
It was the silence of the Canyon.
Everyone was still.
It felt as if the whole world had stopped,
for this enchanting moment.
My imagination was in control of me now.
I could picture so much,
stood in these rocks of history.
So much had happened here.
It made my worries, my life, seem insignificant.
The sun had fallen.
It left behind a spectrum of colours.
To remind people of the beauty our planet can produce.
So fortunate was I to see this natural display,
that I will treasure it so very much.

Ella Selwood (15)
Stratford High School

Stormy Skies

Firmament ripping, electric flashing blue.
Never have I seen such a vivid hue.
I watch entranced, from behind the curtain,
Thunderous crashing: the gods are stamping
Lightning tearing the earth apart.
Instantly followed by nature's percussion at its greatest
Slowly-spaced between flash and thunder.
Counting longer every time
Storm is ebbing, further away
Still I stand and count - hoping for another bout.
But no - gone to far-off places
Giving others spellbound faces.

Lisa Griffiths (14)
Stratford High School

Spellbound

The light was bright
And in the sky
The shape was strange
And up quite high
I couldn't move
Like in a trance
My eyes were blurred
At every glance
But what it was
I never found
I could never tell
I was spellbound.

Nikki Jennings (12)
Stratford High School

My Magical Island

I dream of a special, peaceful, magical island,
A quiet island far away, where I can go to rest,
I'm in my own dreamy world, where no one else can reach me,
A world that only I can reach at any time I like, I look over my enchanting, restful world,
Waves silently sway against the glistening, smooth rocks on the shore,
The shining, warm sun reflects off my face,
Not a cloud can be seen in the glistening blue colour of the sky.
Palm trees' branches swaying from side to side,
A fruit calmly falls from a high branched tree nearby,
I run my fingers through the soft, silky sands,
It feels so warm and soft against my skin.
A light breeze rose to ripple the soft calm sea,
I stand up and feel the warmth of the sea breeze against me,
Slowly I take tiny steps to the silvery shore,
My feet reach the wet polished waves of the shallow, silvery, dark blue sea.
A small fish swims gently by,
The white, calm waves, can be heard.
I reach down to touch the warmth of the magical sea,
I look up to hear the sweet sound of a small bird crying out to its mother,
The strong bright light of the sun gleams across my face into my eyes,
Suddenly I look down to see my magical island is fading,
The silvery ripples of the sea meet together, leaving me on the sandy shore.
I don't want to wake up and leave this world, I want to stay for longer,
Why do I have to leave so soon?
I'll come back to my enchanting, secret, dream island soon . . .

Becky Caden (14)
Stratford High School

SPELLBOUND

I watch as, gently
The great ball of fire
Comes into view over the green,
Dewy hills and,
Golden topped trees.
As I continue to watch,
The sun rolls further into my sight,
Like a golf ball gently being putted into a hole,
Gracing the hills with a warm golden glow
Which makes you glow inside.
I can see it in its entirety now,
And the whole sky is orange,
Birds silhouetting the brilliance as they fly
From the trees,
Greeting each other on this glorious day.
It is higher and more yellow,
Like sand,
Golden on a hot summer's day.
It brings out the green leaves from the tall,
Magnificent trees.
The yellow scattered along the verge
From the daffodils,
And the silver shimmer on the fence
From the spider webs, highlighted
By the dew sparkling in the light
Emitted by the great ball of fire,
The sun.

Nicola Sach (14)
Stratford High School

HOME

Home is where you can cry when you have been hurt emotionally.
Home is where you can enjoy Christmas with your family.
Home is where you can watch the faces of your brothers and sisters when they open their presents.
Home is where you can watch television.
Home is where you love one another.
Home is where your love and care is.
Home is where you can have a friend no one else can see.
Home is where you can have a casual conversation.
Home is where you can talk to your parents about something you cannot tell anyone else.
Home is where you share most of your secrets and all your feelings.
Home is somewhere you can let all your anger out.
Home is where you can enjoy yourself most of the time.
Home is where you feel more secure than you do anywhere else.
Home is where you belong.
My home is for me.

Gareth Ridgley (12)
Stratford High School

DAYDREAMING

A lady is dreaming as she is cleaning
A flock of sheep baa non-stop
As a spaceship landed with a flop
Out came something with three eyes, three heads and three feet
The lady Linda walked up and said 'There is someone I would like you to meet.'
So she led the creature to her mum
But lady Linda looked very glum
To see her mum had fallen on her bum.

Amiee Cotterill (12)
Stratford High School

WATER

Water is calm
Water is clean
A big flowing river
A small trickling stream.

Swans glide on the water
graceful and white
While ducks, look for food
they squabble and fight.

Rain pouring down
the river soon floods
overflowing its banks
and churning up mud.

Night-time approaches clouds move away
the water calms down at the end of the day.
The water's reflection is a beautiful sight
as it ripples and sparkles in the moonlit night.

David Podmore (11)
Stratford High School

COMPUTER MADNESS

My computer sparkles
As I turn it on

The controller cold and hard
The buttons press in like a wet sponge

My computer is magical, charismatic, enchantment
It seems to suck me in
And turns my eyes square.

Michael Wood (11)
Stratford High School

Gran

'Hello love, how are you?
You've grown'
She says as she hugs at my cheek.
Next come the kisses,
Slimy, slippery, slobbering lips.
By the time she's finished,
I'm covered in lipstick.

She waddles into the living room,
And slumps down into an armchair,
The chair squeaks with her weight.
She shouts out, '*Pressies!*'
I groan with reluctance,
As she pulls out a lime green sweater.
My stomach turns,
And I get evil looks from my mother.

One arm of the jumper is longer than the other.
I smile with dread
As she grabs me,
And squeezes me lifeless.
Well, I say to myself,
After all, she is my
Gran.

Scott Redhead (13)
Stratford High School

Waves

Glittery wispy waves in motion,
Splashing rolling waves go crashing,
Vicious water turning like a wheel,
Flapping washing sparkling like glitter.

Dark blue, light blue swirling around,
White and creamy like whipped cream,
Deep and spacious like a bottomless pit,
It mesmerises me and I stare.

Ian Terry (12)
Stratford High School

THE WELLINGTONS

First I was on the top shelf of a shop
Now I am tatty, shiny I'm not.
All I do now is sit around bored
Apart from spring, autumn and winter.

In the spring I go for a walk
Crunch, crunch the sound of the leaves,
In the autumn I'm used again
For conker-picking and walking through leaves.

In winter I have lots of fun
Though I do get cold at times,
Snow I hear the people say
Then I dream how much it is.

I have to go in a tub sometimes
Because I get soggy and muddy.

They always take me to bonfire night
I see pretty patterns,
Reds, blues, yellows and greens
All the colours that please me.

I'm sitting here really bored
'Mum can we get the wellies?'
Here we go again.

Gemma Gold (11)
Stratford High School

Gang Of Girls

All is quiet
All is still
Everything is normal
Until . . .
Here they are
Here they come
Boys rush to doors and windows
Mouths wide open.
You can hear the clonking of high heel shoes
Like horses hooves coming towards you.
There they are
Just in sight
Long blonde hair
Curly and flat
Lipstick all over their mouths.
It's disgraceful
If I dressed like that when I was young I would have got the belt
Say old ladies to themselves.
Just then
Oh my gosh
Ha ha ha
Splish, splash, splosh.
One girl just fell over into a puddle
Everyone laughs
Oh what fun
Serves her right
She runs off home
Do you think she will ever wear high heel shoes again?
I don't!

Jodie Vest (11)
Stratford High School

The Sensational Skirmish

The fielders are like soldiers in battle,
The wicket keeper, like sentry of the stumps,
Batsman, all like heroes, Batman and Robin,
Bowler, thundering cannon, charging in.

Warwickshire, our champions, on the sacred ground of Lords.
Worcestershire, the victors like mighty minotaurs.
The crowd, like a glorious army, cheering on the troops,
Flock like birds round food bars,
Or in the stand in giant groups.

The weather cold and rainy stopped play, but not for long.
The coaches like colonels spurring on the teams.
The day was over we lost the fight,
But it was better than a dream.

Stewart Crow (11)
Stratford High School

Water

Water, water everywhere.
Sometimes roaring,
Sometimes raging,
Sometimes slow and dancing.
Quiet and silky like
Sometimes blue, red, black, brown
Used in a car-wash and iron,
A washing machine and fridge.
Water, water everywhere.

Nicholas Osman (11)
Stratford High School

Spellbound

Snow is pure white,
Untouched, thick, obscure,
A freezing ice-cold blanket,
Which covers the ground.

It feels so thick yet it's so fine,
Falling in patterns so delicate, so gentle,
So little but later so much,
Each so different and unique like a newborn baby.

Outside, so good, your foot leaves a print,
A thick rich ball of snow is thrown,
Everyone enjoys the soft white cotton wool,
But tomorrow it's gone!

Simon Walton (11)
Stratford High School

That Forest

Water running, gushing, rushing down a stream;
Feeding life to the great forest.
Birds chirping, feeding on succulent cherries.
Foxes having a habit of feeding on berries,
And burping after a tasty rabbit.
Deer eating the fresh green grass
With a shining coat like the shade of brass.
Insects squirming, worming their way through life.
The sun starts to go down.
Crackling, shattering lightning streaking across the sky.
Badger fighting until the end of the storm.
Then another day is reborn in that forest.

Adam Martin (11)
Stratford High School

A SHEEP (BAA)

I wish I were a sheep,
Just standing in a field,
Passing the time of day,
And if someone asked me,
'Where is your car?' or
'Which one's your grandma?'
I would simply answer
'Ba, baa or baaa!'

I would enjoy being sheared
(now I haven't got a beard)
I like the farmer too
(though he's gone a bit na noo)
If I chose a method of transport
It would be by limousine,
'Cause taking us around in an old rust cart
Is certainly just obscene.

I don't like being rounded up
It's just a waste of time
If that dog barks at me again
I'll give him the V sign!

I wish I were a sheep
Passing the time of day.
The only thing that troubles me
Is eating bales of hay!

Oliver Stewart (13)
Stratford High School

In The Eyes Of A Cat

I know a cat nearby
and he likes to look at me.
His evil eyes half-closed like shutters,
his whiskers like strands of grass
blowing in the wind.
His black and white coat
it's his pride and joy!

Sometimes he is happy,
Sometimes he is sad,
Even when he's hungry
he can still be bad.

Although he may look cute,
with his little pink nose,
and light footsteps
be warned, he has a bite!

Katie Walter (11)
Stratford High School

Thirsty, Thirsty

Not long ago I felt very thirsty,
The more that I drank the more I felt thirsty.

So I told my mum who looked in a book,
She made an appointment with the doctor to have a look.

I went to the doctor the very next day, who said 'I was fine,
just going through a phase.'

So that was that and I went away.

Claire May (12)
Stratford High School

Queen Of Hearts

My heart is empty,

Deep inside it really hurts,
The news was terrible, shocking and bad.

Her life is over, but it is not.
She's my queen forever more.

Her sons were shocked, sad with pain,
The world was quiet for those she helped
and saved and for herself.

But when I say these words that were trapped inside,
I feel she's still out there helping those who need it.

Melantha Thomson (12)
Stratford High School

The Sea

Little sailing boats bobbing up and down on the horizon,
Speedboats whizzing across the shore,
Nice clean water with snorklers in,
Kids shouting and playing in the sea,
Surfers coming in-shore on the crashing waves,
Little kids' boats getting blown back in.

Whales catching their prey,
Boat wrecks getting washed in,
Waves crashing over the shore,
The sea can be fun but it can be vicious.

David Eburah (11)
Stratford High School

SPELLBOUND

I was driving in my blue car,
When a spaceship came from afar,
It landed in two farmers' fields,
Five Martians came out with their shields.
I was entranced, surprised, spellbound,
At what I had seen and found,
I was astonished and amazed,
But almost definitely dazed.
Each one had six different arms,
They were all very, very calm,
They were a beautiful bright green,
And extraordinarily clean.
The aliens walked on their hands,
Round about on earth's great lands,
My car stopped, I sat in a stare,
They seemed kind, gentle, mild and to care.
The hairs on my neck stood upright,
And they gave me a fright,
As they came closer I fainted,
When I woke up they had painted,
My car a truly gross green,
They had also given it a clean.
'Are you human? We come in peace,
So please, do not call the police.'
I couldn't explain what I'd seen,
I was spellbound at that scene,
I have witnessed real aliens.

Ingram Hazel (12)
Stratford High School

SOMETIMES

Sometimes I wonder is life worth living?
Sometimes I wonder am I worth it?
The news always broadcasts the bad, never the good
Hurricanes, poverty, earthquakes too
I just hope nothing happens to you.

Sometimes I wonder are all people friendly?
Sometimes I wonder am I safe where I am?
You always read about tragedies, I just hope they are few,
So I hope nothing happens to you.

Sometimes I wonder will earth be here long?
Sometimes I wonder will earth soon be gone?
You always hear about the hole in the sky.
I hope it will never affect us.

Lydia Burton (12)
Stratford High School

SHEEP

Sheep, sheep I have four sheep,
Sheep, sheep they lie in a heap.
They are like a cloud with four legs,
Bleating sheep, sleeping sheep.
Rolling in muck, eating in the barn
Spot, Rolley, Smelly and Fluffy
All fat and round like a fluffy bit of fluff.
They walk slow, slower and even slower,
Some like to ride on their mother's back
And some are clever enough to put on a hat.
Sheep, sheep, I love my sheep.

Natalie Kemp (11)
Stratford High School

The Fair

Today is the day,
I'll go to the fair,
Candyfloss, popcorn,
And action is there.
I've been waiting and waiting,
With anticipation,
For all of the fun,
And exhilaration.
I lose track of the time,
And I think that it's seven,
I look at my watch,
It's now gone eleven!
The laughter and games,
The hum of the crowds,
I don't want to go home,
Excitement abounds.

Jemma Caldwell (13)
Stratford High School

Weather

Whether the sun is shining in the sky,
Whether the rain is falling, pattering on the window,
Whether the lightning flashes, like a knife coming through the air,
Whether the snow is falling, melting into the ground,
Whether the colourful rainbow is shining in the sky,
Weather is all around us,
Everywhere!

Timothy Woolley (11)
Stratford High School

Autumn And Me

As the memories of the summer fade into the mysterious mist,
The dawn of autumn peeps over the dark hill of dead border plants,
from the hot summer.
Virginia creeper turns the colour of a sunset, of bright reds and oranges.

The maple leaves bob up and down in the cold wind, like a crowd
of football fans in a silent stadium.
Twisted willow tree, stands still and lonely, by the school path.
Hazel-coloured conkers, look like they have been polished for
a hundred days.
The ground feels hard and forgotten, it's raining leaves they're
everywhere.

Dappled shadows from the tall strong trees.
In the evening sitting, listening, waiting for the birds to take their rest.
For quiet to think about yourself and things.
How autumn is relaxing to me,
Squirrels are busy doing something or other.
Cats busy catching mice.
But autumn is busy being autumn.

Phoebe English (11)
Stratford High School

Spiders!

They creep in the night
Giving you a fright!
Their big, long, black, hairy legs stretch out in front of them.
Weaving a web round and round
Catching flies as if they were fishing
Webs glisten in the sun.
Raindrops falling and falling down and down on their web.

Sophie Leow-Dyke (11)
Stratford High School

Autumn

Autumn day when cold and frost comes.
Golden leaves falling from the trees.
Frost and cold make me shiver and make me
chill like mad.
Autumn winds blow my hat up a tree so high
and makes me red as a rose.
Coat and gloves, hat and scarves makes me warm inside.
My face cold as ice.
Icy days make me slip.
My feet feel like a block of ice.
Golden leaves blow in a round circle.
Squirrels running up trees and hiding in a hole.
Shiny conkers falling from trees with their green
prickly shells dropping on the ground.
Squirrels running back and forwards collecting
nuts to eat in their holes.
Autumn days are fun to play in all day.

Sian Haggitt (11)
Stratford High School

Water

Water rushing and gushing and gurgling.
Water is the main thing in our life.
Water can be still or rough.
Water sparkles like a star.
We all like water and we like having a wash in it.
The water is lovely and we drink water.
The water sounds like a swoosh when it moves.
Where would we be without *water*?

Aaron Aston (11)
Stratford High School

THE SNAIL

A snail went into the woods one night,
Hoping not to get frost bite.
On and on went the snail,
Leaving behind a slippery trail.
Looking at it from a hole,
Lay a little baby mole.
Looking up into the trees,
The snail saw some red berries.
The wind is blowing with all its might,
Making the trees sway left and right.
Soon the morning was here,
This gave the snail lots of cheer.
Then the snail left the woods,
And entered a dewy wet field.

Steven Perkins (11)
Stratford High School

OUTSIDE MY WINDOW

I look out of my window,
I see so much,
Like my next-door neighbour's garden.
I see mine as well.
The colours I see,
Green, pinks, browns a lot more.
All the autumn colours.
Trees swaying,
Leaves gushing,
I hear the wind whistling,
Outside,
As I look out my window.

Sara Franklin (12)
Stratford High School

CLUMSY

Crash! Smash! Bang!
Whoops!
A feeling like someone's punched you in the stomach
On no not *that* vase
The one which mum made for gran and grandad
The one which is so precious we can't even use it.
My head turns empty
A slow shiver goes down my spine
I turn cold and I feel alone
No one will stick up for me, not this time.

'Siân, what have you done?'
Asks the sharp, suspicious mother's voice.
'My vase!' she cries
I know what she'll say it keeps going round inside my head.

'No more pocket money'
She shouts as if she's about to cry.

I've really hurt her I know I have
I feel guilty
I felt ashamed
If something gets broken
It's true I always commit the crime
It's never my brother
It's me all the time.

Siân Walters (13)
Stratford High School

JUNE

A pale blue street lay above.
A sky with no clouds to be seen.
Shining down, a golden beam.
Rises
The earth acting as a sponge.
Absorbing the pursuing heat from above.

Far away I hear playing of carefree children.
Having fun.
No more school.
Giggling, laughing, screaming,
Smiling and chatting.
Why does life change?

The birds singing, tweeting,
In joyous frenzy above.
Arched willows overlook,
Protecting the damp grass.
As a soundless breeze blows past.

Meandering close by,
Glistening in the sunlight, like a mirror,
Rests a stream.
Surrounding.
I smell the aroma of the morning dew,
Newly mowed,
Among which peak through flowers.
Blue violets, tiny plants.
Roses that make the world so sweet.
And bring such joy in *June.*

Becky Tucker (13)
Stratford High School

FUTURE EARTH

In the good old days when the lands were green,
And all the world was nice and clean.
I was proud of you as a race,
You put a smile upon my face.
We all lived together in harmony,
The plants, the animals, you and me.

Now destruction fed by your greed,
And taking more than you could possibly need,
Has forced my arteries to clog,
And covered me in awful smog.
The warnings were there,
But did you care?
Slash and burn,
You didn't learn,
You've blown your chance,
I'm on my last dance.

Don't say you'll do something straight away,
It should have been yesterday not today.
The time has passed it doesn't wait,
And now today is just *too late, too late, too late, too late . . .*

Martin Baxter (11)
Stratford High School

AUTUMN

The season has come,
The trees are tall,
And all the conkers are starting to fall.
The leaves are gold, the leaves are brown,
And I can see them on the ground.

The autumn wind in my face,
And I can hear it all over the place.
Here comes the harvest night,
It gets so cold it gives me a fright.
The harvest moon is very bright,
It blinds my eyes if I look up at night.

Benjamin Skinner (11)
Stratford High School

SNOW

So white and light,
Covering everything from sight.
Like icing on a cake.
The trees are like decorations.
The snow sprinkling down,
Like salt from a salt shaker.
Each little flake, so individual,
Yet so alike.

It's so peaceful and calm,
As if time had stopped.
The feeling of contentment,
And excitement.
So cold yet the feeling of
Warmth inside.
So cold yet everything,
Smells so fresh.
Being out there makes you
Feel a part of it,
As though it was another world.

Alicia Leow-Dyke (15)
Stratford High School

DROWNING

Trapped in a new terrifying world
With no air around you
Desperately trying to escape
But you're helpless
There's nothing you can do.

Your mind goes blank
Knowing it's the end
There's nothing to see
Nothing to hear
Going deeper
Getting darker
It's gone.

Waking up being able to breathe
Fresh air around me
All sunny and bright
Feeling free and complete!

Johanna Holdsworth (13)
Stratford High School

AUTUMN

Autumn days and autumn nights
all the days feel good and bright
until one day is really glum
autumn has become.

All the trees have lost their leaves,
fruit is nice and sweet to eat.
I can smell a hot apple pie
then I look up into the sky.

Shorter days and longer nights,
everybody has lost their kites
in the strong wind.
Everybody knows that it blows and blows,
but never goes.

Amanda Keech (11)
Stratford High School

WHAT A WONDERFUL DREAM

I lay in my bed with many thoughts in my head,
silent and still hearing the rain run down my window-sill.

My eyes start to close and my mind starts to wonder,
I can just see pure blackness, my body drifts
peacefully up into the silent air of the starry night.

I suddenly pick up fast speed, the brightness of the
stars scalds my eye.
What's this I see, could it be, am I here in the world
of the unknown?

I come across planets at very fast speed,
all different shapes and sizes.

That will be all for me, I've seen what I want to see,
I travel back to the world of normality,
with lots of strength I open my eyes and see my posters above me.

What a wonderful dream I have come across,
just what I wanted to dream.

Katie Chandler (13)
Stratford High School

It's That Time Of Year

We go to the Mop, it comes once a year
Everyone goes, some with a fear.
I like to go on all the rides, so I take plenty of money
Which my Mum does not think is funny.
We all have a go on things to win
Fluffy teddies, sweets and balloons.
It's very busy, everyone shouting and pushing,
We go with friends, in the dark, it is fun.
All the music and the bright lights.
The smell of the hot dogs is always there.
We all go round, friends and all.
We're all dizzy, we hope we don't fall.
We all like to eat, our lovely food
We all go home in a very good mood.

Kelly Millward (13)
Stratford High School

Blackness

It was as still as the lull before the storm.
A moist dew settles on the lawn.
A gentle breeze sends the dried-up leaves
from the old oak spiralling to the floor.
The Victorian canal disappears from sight
and an evil mist hovers on the scene.
It moves in closer, much closer.
I feel a sense of falling
Then a rush of water.
Blackness.

Chris Wood (13)
Stratford High School

What's It Like?

What would it be like to die
To rise up to heaven and fly?
Will it be good,
Will it be bad,
Will it be happy
Or will it be sad?

Will I go to heaven
Or will I go to hell?
This is the question that no one can tell.

I want to know how I'll go
Will it be happy I just don't know.
These are questions that no one can answer,
I'll just have to wait till my life is over.

Gemma Hawkins (13)
Stratford High School

Friends

Friends are the best,
Without them we would all be lost.
Rare special friends are hard to find.
In a friendship there must be trust.
Every friend is special to me in some way.
New or old, I will never forget them.
Daring or not you are still my friend.
Sometimes I'm sad and you cheer me up.
Having friends is everything you can wish for.
I'd hate to have no friends.
No one to share my problems.
Perfect pals forever.

Zoe Russon (13)
Stratford High School

FLYING

What would it be like to fly?
Soaring among sponge-like clouds,
playing games in the air,
seeing the world below me
like a patchwork quilt.
The broccoli trees cushioning my fall.
Swooping in the wind, free as a bird.

What would it be like to fly?
Weaving among the other birds,
up in the deep expanse of my new world,
spreading across the world below.
Like an ocean still, yet full of life.
The never-ending path before me,
waiting to be explored.
Oh, what would it be like to fly?

Martha Welch (13)
Stratford High School

FIREWORKS

Dazzling, sparkling, shimmering
The illuminations of colours.
Red, green, silver
The Catherine wheel spinning like a washing machine.

The rockets belting up to the sky
Boom!
It makes me jump!
The glitter is cascading
Sparklers are swishing in the air
Beautiful patterns everywhere.
Pretty.

Gemma Crow (13)
Stratford High School

Tammy!

Tammy is a collie, brown, black and white.
Running, walking and sleeping every single night.
Our friendship will last forever and ever.
I hope we will always be together.
Although she has gone to another place,
I will never forget that friendly face.
She had a birthday like our very own,
She used to get excited, and receive a large bone.
She used to love water, we used to have fun,
We used to play together in the hot sun.
Every week we'd have a shopping spree,
Mainly for Tammy, never me.
She'd bark if you stamped upon the ground,
or even made the slightest sound.
Why did she go please tell me why?
She's still in my life as a star in the sky.

Lisa Grasby (13)
Stratford High School

Autumn

Leaves fall from the tree.
Coloured golden they must be.
The squirrels come and eat the nuts,
That have fallen from the tree.
People go and collect the conkers,
That have fallen on the floor.
Combine harvesters start to roar
As they cut and churn some more.
As the fog clears the leaves are dead,
As I see a new blossom's head.

Joe Evans (11)
Stratford High School

AUTUMN

Autumn is coming, leaves begin to fall.
The days and nights get colder.
Squirrels come and play.
Look outside and see the frost
and all of the conkers in the compost.
As you step outside for some fresh air
a chill will shiver down your spine.
Your nose will go red and your toes will go numb
and the mist and the fog gather together.
Cold strong winds blow red and golden leaves
across the pavements.
Icy roads and frosty gardens.
Harvest corn and bright bright moons.
Trees are bare and birds are cold.
Poor dead flowers lie dead on the ground.
The days get shorter and the nights get longer.
You see cold hungry cats outside.
You sit on a chair and look outside at the cars
that go by and you wish you could go and play in the leaves.
You drink lots of hot soup hoping it will warm you up.
You can see lots of paw-prints leading to the top of your garden.

Laura Collins (11)
Stratford High School

AUTUMN

Here comes autumn. Yes! Yes! Yes!
It is truly my season best.
I see leaves gold and brown,
I can see them on the ground.
The autumn winds blow here and there,
In my face and everywhere.

Winds scare me every night,
It gives me such a big, big fright.
Everywhere I look around,
There's dead flowers on the ground,
Here comes autumn. Yes! Yes ! Yes!
It is truly my season best.

Sam Lee (11)
Stratford High School

Music

Music is everywhere.
Both happy or sad
Loud or soft
You can rave or smooch
Whatever the mood
Or just listen
Alone or in a group
Different instruments can be played
Like strings and wood
Brass and drums
Each country has its own special style
From the didgeridoo down under
To the pipes of the Celts
Each has its own special anthem
Like God Save The Queen, Marseillaise
Many go in search of fame
Just drawn to the glamour of pop
Also many bands go in search of No 1
With great songs to be sung
My mum likes classical
I prefer pop
But then she's old
and I'm not.

Hannah Wilson (13)
Stratford High School

AUTUMN

Autumn is that time of year,
Which bring leaves and conkers,
Wheat, fruit all those kinds of things
come falling from the trees.
So cover up those knees.
First of all your nose goes red,
now you'll be running to your Dad's wooden shed.
Leaves go a golden brown,
all down the streets of London town,
the mist is coming thicker and thicker.
Oh dear me, I have a cold, I have to get rid of it even quicker.
Winds are going faster than ever,
it will be the harvest moon,
the animals will be collecting up their nuts soon.
Mice, hedgehogs, badgers too,
all sorts of animals but not cows which go moo.
Autumn is that time of year
so you may see lots of deer.

Esther Foster (11)
Stratford High School

THE SEASONS

The seasons start, and spring is warm
Leaves start to form on the trees
Animals come out of hibernation,
With all the insects and bees.

Next is summer, which can be hot
We're very glad when it's here.
You can do so much in summer,
It's a great time of the year.

Then autumn arrives
The temperature drops
The trees become bare
And we harvest the crops.

Winter is last
Dark nights form
Bad weather then follows,
And we wrap up warm.

Elizabeth Blewer (13)
Stratford High School

AUTUMN!

Autumn is a time of year, that's cold with lots of colours,
Golds, yellows and lots of reds, but without a lot of flowers!
Flowers die in the autumn you see,
Because of the cold, which chills me!

In the autumn you can see,
All the leaves fall on me!
If you do go out don't forget your coat,
You certainly won't be able to go on a boat!
All the water's covered in ice,
It's really cold and not very nice!

On horse chestnut trees there are conkers,
Watch they don't fall and make you bonkers!
With a shorter day and a longer night,
Really early you lose the light!

You won't see many animals about,
They're all asleep so please don't shout!
Autumn is a time of year, that's cold with lots of colours,
Golds, yellows and lots of reds, but without a lot of flowers!

Hannah Whatcott (11)
Stratford High School

Autumn Days

Autumn days are on their way,
the squirrels are scurrying down the trees and land on a
bunch of nice soft leaves.
As the days go shorter and the nights grow longer,
you will wake up to a chill,
where your nose will go red and your feet will go numb,
and you see all the frost on the floor.
You make your way to school, through the mist and the fog,
and you see all the conkers on the roadside.
You see all the flowers lying dead on the floor,
where the frost has been and attacked them.
You get out of the car and you feel the wind so greatly that
you get a shiver down your spine.
You've had your day at school.
You're lying in your bed thinking about how autumn came to be,
then suddenly you're disturbed by some rattling outside.
You see a squirrel outside and think 'Autumn must be nice
for squirrels, all the food, nuts and all.'
You go downstairs and rush outside to see the squirrel, but it's gone.
You head back in, and see your cat at the doorway putting its paws
on the floor very wearily.
You go back in and say 'Mum, it's nice, autumn, isn't it?'

Liane Garside (11)
Stratford High School

Lottery Madness

I want to win, I have to win
I'll buy a ticket
Oh no! My ticket, I lost it in that thicket
Oh look! My luck is in, here's a pin!
I'll pick it up and look! It's my ticket.

Later, the Lottery's on!
I've got to win!
Where's that pin?
Wow all three balls!
I think I've won!

Robbie Parker (13)
Stratford High School

An Autumn Day

It's 8 o'clock.
The harsh chill of the morning
is melted.
By the misty autumn sun
waking up to greet the world.

It's 11 o'clock.
Screaming kids
in wellington boots
shuffle through mountains of leaves
and harassed mothers trudge
with overladen shopping bags.

It's 4 o'clock.
The watery sun is just beginning to fade
behind the rustling oak trees.
Only the bonfire builders are out
finishing their day's work.

It's 8 o'clock.
The smell of autumn is still in the air.
Damp leaves and bonfire smoke.
The sun has disappeared
leaving only the trees to whisper
and the fireworks to light the sky.

Amy Wein (14)
Stratford High School

AUTUMN

Autumn is really fun.
You'll never be glum.
If you collect conkers,
You'll never go bonkers.
If you run through the leaves,
You won't fall on your knees.
Autumn has shorter days and longer nights,
That really gives me a fright.
The frosts make me chilly,
That makes me feel silly.
The winds,
Are like dolphins' fins.
You can watch mice,
Trying to slide on the ice.

Kerry Ford (11)
Stratford High School

AUTUMN

On an autumn's day the conkers fall.
On an autumn's day winds blow.
On an autumn's day leaves rustle.
On an autumn's day squirrels climb the big oak tree.
On an autumn's day picking conkers off the ground.
On an autumn's day watching the sun set.
On an autumn's night seeing Venus and Mars.
On an autumn's day the combine harvesters churn some more.
On an autumn's day the fog clambers across the road.
On an autumn's day sun has risen to see the beautiful buds.

On an autumn's day . . .

Stephen Devey (11)
Stratford High School

AUTUMN

As I watch the golden sunlight pouring
through the trees,
I can see the crispy leaves dancing in the breeze.

Autumn days when the winds are cold,
And the frost covers the fields.

I can just sit there and watch the beautiful
harvest grow and yield.

Autumn brings chills and thrills, all mixed together.
Autumn, I wish would last forever and ever.

The greens and reds and all the colours
In my head, brings me a lovely smell of
Autumn.

Hayley Ash (12)
Stratford High School

HORSES

Horses are black but cannot go quack,
Horses are brown but cannot wear a crown,
Horses are white but they are not a knight,
Horses are grey but cannot say hey!
Horses are patchy but they cannot catch me,
Horses are the colour dun but like a good run,
Horses can be found on muddy ground,
Horses can also be found near dry ground,
Horses gallop around the tall tree and gallop through the leaves,
Horses are the colour dapple and they are really like apples.

Rachel Day (11)
Stratford High School

AUTUMN

Autumn leaves begin to fall,
All the trees look really tall,
All the leaves that have fallen down,
Go a really crispy coloured brown.

Autumn is the time of year,
When the wind whistles it's all you hear,
People all start to get a cold,
More tissues are getting sold.

Days are getting short,
Nights are getting long,
The people start practising,
Some new harvest songs.

Mornings are getting full of mist and fog,
You could see people walking their dog,
Towards the fields they go,
The grass is cut really low.

The leaves are full of colours,
Like red, gold and yellow,
You sometimes hear people bellow,
They sometimes say hello.

Kelly Nicholls (11)
Stratford High School

THAT GHOSTLY TREE ON THAT GHOSTLY HILL

That ghostly tree on that ghostly hill,
Haunts me every night,
Its rickety old branches wave around at me,
As if it's coming to give me a fright.

That old hole in the middle of it,
It seems so strange and weird.
As if a strange monster lives in it,
Who eats things which look like frozen beards!

One strange night on that ghostly hill,
Some owls sat on all of the branches.
I watched them all gather into a circle,
Then they all sat down and did something called 'larches'.

Larches is where lots of birds gather round,
They sing songs about old rickety trees,
But they came to this particular one,
To whistle about it in the breeze.

There in that hole there was actually a monster,
He was watching this with his red eyes.
He was hoping to catch them,
Then eat them like they were your favourite flavoured pie!

Then the next night a magician came,
He said a strange sounding spell.
It made the tree make very strange noises,
Which made it disappear quicker than some strange smells.

That ghostly tree on that ghostly hill,
Won't haunt me anymore.
Its rickety branches might come to you,
Haunting you now forever more.

Sophie Lemberger (11)
Stratford High School

ON AN AUTUMN DAY

I woke up on an autumn day.
I got up then I shivered straight away.
I got dressed and had some breakfast,
I went out.
There was frost on the grass in the garden.
I noticed I was walking on a bed of conkers.
The trees were all bare.
With a bed of leaves lying all over the ground,
I walked on them.
They crunched and crackled as I stepped.
Two squirrels raced from a tree to the stream
which trickled all the time,
like a fountain very softly.
It started to get dark at about 6.00pm.
It started to get cold and then I shivered.
I started to walk back home.
I saw the bare trees.
Then I started to trip up over the conkers,
and went back home.

Phillip Camp (11)
Stratford High School

AUTUMN

Autumn is a time of year
When winter is very near.
Shorter days and longer nights,
Frost that really bites.

Squirrels jump around the trees and leaves begin to fall,
Combine harvester wanders by as it cuts the corn.
People celebrate harvest time with their wheat and corn,
As wind outside blows, blows against the door.

Conkers fall and hit people on the head,
By flowers which are dead.
Ice has fallen on the pond,
Where people ice-skate rather long.

Autumn has nearly gone,
And winter is really here,
So I'll say goodbye
And I'll see you next year.

Helen Goodman (11)
Stratford High School

When Darkness Comes

The dog is barking at the window,
What's out there?
I won't look,
I can't.

The room is full of emptiness,
No colour,
No life,
Just darkness.

The now darkened posters spread around the room.
Each figure fixing its eyes on me.
I close my eyes, in order to escape eye contact.
But it's no use,
They still stare.

There is no sound,
Just silence,
But then, what is it?
There's creaking on the landing, but everyone's in bed.
It's my imagination, it must be.

Sara Casley (13)
Stratford High School

THE BULLY IS BEATEN

Go home Ginger,
You don't belong.
It's the colour of your hair,
It's stupid, it's wrong!

The bully lunged forward,
He tried to punch Ginger.
Ginger swerved,
He did not linger.

The bully fell,
He crashed to the ground,
And then from Ginger,
Came a rather timid sound.

'It was your fault!'
Ginger cried,
Get up off the ground,
And get back inside!

Tom Cox (13)
Stratford High School

AUTUMN

In autumn the frosts land on the trees with golden leaves.
As squirrels play with conkers and nuts.
If a nut falls in a patch of sleeping flowers,
all squirrels will come and have fun.
The howling winds carry the cold in and out the wheat
and children are sad because school is back.
In the night you can see Venus and Mars in the sky.
You can also see the harvest moon.

Michael Scowcroft (11)
Stratford High School

MEMORIES

The night crawls on, now the day is gone,
The moon shines on, now the sun is gone.
I long for the sun to come,
The sun rises casting rays of light on nearby clouds.
Suddenly the silence is broken,
Nearby an alarm clock goes off
In a crescendo of sound.
Silence, except for someone's nearby cough.
Rain crashes on the roof,
Down the gutter goes the rain,
Down into the nearby drain.
I lift my pillow and look for my tooth.
There lies some money in its place,
I call my parents, say it's proof,
I was very sure my dream was true,
That there was a tooth fairy living in my shoe.

When I was young I believed in many things,
Santa Claus, fairies and horses with wings.
I don't believe in these any more,
But the other day I swear I saw
A tooth fairy sitting by my door.

Joanne Dyer (13)
Stratford High School

DARKNESS

Pitch black and silence all around,
Still, creepy, scary, I'm terrified.
A sound screams out but where from?
I run but where to?
Silence comes once more and calm with it,
I realise it was just an owl screeching.
My eyes become accustomed to the darkness,
I see familiar shapes especially my front door.
My heartbeat starts to calm down,
It slowly stops its heavy pound.
Home at last, the lights burn bright,
No longer in darkness of evil at the dead of night.

Gemma Newby (13)
Stratford High School

AUTUMN

In autumn there is lots of fruit.
Fruit for all the animals.
Shorter days mean less to do.
A squirrel scavenges for conkers.
As the leaves start to fall
They turn a yellowy gold,
as they shine in the moonlight.
As the wind gets colder
we all dress up warmer.
With all the leaves on the floor
all we hear is a crunch.

Michael Bush (11)
Stratford High School

SKY!

My dog Sky is a Labrador cross,
She always want to be the boss.
She likes to walk but loves to run,
She loves to lie beneath the sun.
She loves her birthday when it comes around,
She'd bark and bark at the quietest sound.
Chocolate is her favourite food,
She'd always be sad if I were in a mood.
She hates the visits to the vet,
Although she loved it when they first met.
I know inside she loves us all,
She loves it when we throw the ball.
I love her all so much.

Nikola Hamer (13)
Stratford High School

THE LOVE OF MY LIFE

She is beautifully shaped,
She has a great tan,
She can always keep a secret,
And never hurts anyone's feelings,
She always looks great,
Even though she lives outside,
She loves lots of things,
Like birds and trees,
And watches them every day,
I love my garden shed!

Rick Frier (13)
Stratford High School

RAIN!

I sit in my room,
and wait for the rain to cease.
Outside the world is dark,
and full of gloom.
No one is out.
But what would you expect,
for it's thunder and lightning,
and the world is dead.

I listen to the rain,
hitting my window-sill.
Sometimes it's scary,
sometimes it's not.
But when the thunder goes off,
I crawl under the covers,
and hide from the world,
and all its sadness.
For it's only there that I can escape.

Lauren Dyer (13)
Stratford High School

WHAT WOULD IT BE LIKE?

What would it be like to fly
Over the hills into the sky?
Over the moon
Into space
Forgetting about the human race?
Round the galaxy
I'd fly so far
Better than a motor car
Flying round all the stars
Then exploring Jupiter and Mars.

Ruth Woodward (13)
Stratford High School

Just My Cuppa Tea!

When I grow up I want to see and travel the world.
See new things, see different things,
Wow, wouldn't it be so good!
How about America, New Zealand?
No! Not my cuppa tea.
It will have to be somewhere hot,
Corfu!
Hot, sunny and beautiful beaches.
I could meet new people, buy souvenirs
and eat all day.
Then I could move on and go somewhere like Africa.
Yes please! Just my cuppa tea.

When I grow up I want to be an air hostess.
Fly to new places and look at the views.
Wow, wouldn't it be so good!
China, Canada, here I come!
No! Not my cuppa tea.
I want to go to Germany,
Where my Auntie lives - see her again
in her new house.
Then I could move on home.
Yes please! Just my cuppa tea.

Hannah Rowland (13)
Stratford High School